NOTES ON MODERN JAINISM

NOTES ON
MODERN JAINISM
WITH SPECIAL REFERENCE TO THE
SVETAMBARA, DIGAMBARA AND STHANAKAVASI SECTS.

By

Mrs. SINCLAIR STEVENSON, M.A. (T.C.D.)

SOMETIME SCHOLAR OF SOMERVILLE COLLEGE, OXFORD.

GYAN

Published by

Gyan Publishing House
5, Ansari Road
Daryaganj, New Delhi-110002
Phone: 011-47034999, 9811692060
E-mail: books@gyanbooks.com

Distribution Network
gyanbooks.com
India, USA, Canada, UK, Australia, France

ISBN : 978-81-212-6280-4 (PB)
First Published, 1910

2nd Impression 2022

Printed at: Gyan Press, Delhi.

NOTES ON MODERN JAINISM
Author: Mrs. SINCLAIR STEVENSON

NOTES ON
MODERN JAINISM

WITH SPECIAL REFERENCE TO THE S'VETA'MBARA, DIGAMBARA AND STHA'NAKAVA'SI SECTS.

BY

MRS. SINCLAIR STEVENSON, M.A. (T.C.D.)

SOMETIME SCHOLAR OF SOMERVILLE COLLEGE, OXFORD.

1910.

HVNC LIBELLVM DE TRISTI VITAE SEVERITATE CVM MEAE TVM MARITI MATRI MEMORIAE MONVMENTVM DEDICO QVAE EXEMPLVM LONGE ALIVM SECVTAE NOMEN MATERNVM TAM FELICITER ORNAVERVNT.

PREFACE.

THESE notes on Jainism have been compiled mainly from information supplied to me by Gujarāti speaking Jaina, so it has seemed advisable to use the Gujarāti forms of their technical terms.

It would be impossible to issue this little book without expressing my indebtedness to the Rev. G. P. Taylor, D. D., Principal of the Fleming Stevenson Divinity College, Ahmedabad, who placed all the resources of his valuable library at my disposal, and also to the various Jaina friends who so courteously bore with my interminable questionings.

I am specially grateful to a learned Jaina gentleman who read through all the MS. with me, and thereby saved me, I hope, from some of the numerous pitfalls which beset the pathway of anyone who ventures to explore an alien faith.

MARGARET STEVENSON.

Irish Mission,
Rajkot. India.
October 6th, 1909.

CONTENTS

JAINISM.

"JAINISM," says Monsieur A. Barth,* "is one of the least known amongst those [religions] which have performed an important part in the past of India." Dr. Burgess † believes that "research during the last half century has perhaps been less directed to the study of Jainism than to any other branch of Indian study," and it is probably owing to the prevailing ignorance of Jainism that a recent writer‡ has ventured to stigmatise it as "a religion in which the chief points insisted on are that one should deny God, worship man, and nourish vermin," and to such a religion he denies the right even to exist.

This ignorance is all the more surprising when one remembers the great interest which attaches to Jainism as "the only one of the almost primeval mendicant orders which survives in India at the present day," and the contempt so liberally poured forth is scarcely merited by a religious community which has done much to foster the study of language and of science, whose members, though numbering less than a million and a third, are almost the

---

* Barth. Religions of India. p. 140.

† Digambara Jaina Iconography. p. 1. Dr. Burgess goes on to point out that such research as there has been is chiefly directed to the literature of the Swetāmbara sect.

‡ Hopkins. Religions of India. p. 297.

most literate in India,* whose temples are famous amongst the glories of the East, and whose worship far excels in purity of thought and ritual the Hinduism which surrounds it.

Jainism, like its great rival Buddhism, seems to have taken its rise in the sixth century before Christ, an age in which religious speculation was rife in many parts of the world.

In India the joyous, childlike faith reflected in the earlier Vedas had been stifled under priestly domination; "the Aryan Holy land was parcelled out among a number of petty chieftains, who waged internecine war one against another†;" the climate, then as now, exerted its depressing influence on all beneath its sway, and the consequent pessimism is reflected in the philosophies of the times.

The immediate cause which gave rise to both Buddhism and Jainism was probably the caste exclusiveness of the Brāhmans in restricting entrance into the medicant or fourth *āsrama* to members of their own community.‡ This restriction was specially obnoxious to members of the next, the Kṣatriya (or warrior) caste, and it is noticeable that it is from this caste that the historic leaders of both religions sprang, in a part of the world, too, where Brahman influence was already weakening.

---

* Twenty-five per cent of the Jaina are able to read and write; thus they are second only to the Pārsis, of whom two thirds are literate.

† Imperial Gazetteer of India. Vol. I. p. 407.

‡ The old Brahmanic religion directed a man to pass through four successive āsrama (stages), first that of a religious student, next that of a house-holder, then to retire from the world as an anchorite, and lastly to spend the remaining years of his life as a wandering mendicant.

LIFE OF MAHA'VIRA.

Mahāvira, the founder, or (as it would perhaps be more accurate to call him) the reformer, of Jainism, was born about 599 B. C. His antagonism to Brahmanism was marked even before his birth, for we are told in one of the most famous of the Jaina sacred books, the Kalpa Sutra,* that his embryo was removed from the Brāhmaṇi Devānandā to the Kṣatriyāṇi Tris'alā.

His father Siddhārtha was a petty Rājā, the head of the Kṣatriya clan of the Nāta, who lived in Kollāga, a suburb of Vaisāli (the modern Besār), about 27 miles north of Patna. Dr. Hoernle† gives a most interesting account of the government of this place, which seems to have been a sort of oligarchic republic; "its government was vested in a Senate, composed of the heads of the resident Kṣatriya clans, and presided over by an officer who had the title of King and was assisted by a Viceroy and a Commander in chief."

Siddhārtha was married to Tris'alā, the daughter of this republican king, and from the Kalpa Sutra we gain a charming picture of the happy motherhood of the princess. We read of her joy when, through the fourteen wondrous dreams vouchsafed to her in one night, she learnt that she should bear a prophet son, and of her fixed determination not to go to sleep again that night lest any unlucky dreams should mar the effect.‡ Before the child was born "she took her walks in places which were empty and agreeable as well

---

* Sacred Books of the East. Vol. xxii. p. 226.

† Annual Address, Asiatic Society of Bengal, 1898.

‡ S. B. E. xxii. 240.

as delightful to the mind ;" * and at last, when " the sky in all its directions [was] clear, bright and pure ; while a favourable and agreeable low wind swept the earth ; at the time when the fields were green and all people glad... ... ... (Tris'alā,) perfectly healthy herself, gave birth to a perfectly healthy boy." †

His father had already decided what the boy's personal name should be : " From the moment that this our boy has been begotten, our silver increased, our gold increased,...the intensity of our liberality and popularity highly increased. Therefore when this our boy will be born, we shall give him the fit name, attributive and conformable to his quality—Vardhamāna," (i. e ' the increasing one.') ‡

Vardhamāna, or (as he is called in the various Jaina scriptures) Mahāvira, had discovered even before his birth how completely his mother's happiness was bound up in his, and he therefore came to the following decision : " It will not behove me, during the life of my parents, to tear out my hair, and leaving the house to enter the state of houselessness" §; so, unlike Buddha, he lived the ordinary life of a nobleman until his parents' death. He married, and his wife, Yas'ōdā, bore him a daughter, Anojjā (or Priyadars'anā), whose titled husband, Jamāli, later on became one of his followers, and the connections thus formed were all to help him later in his life work. His parents eventually died, having kept all the rules of their religion ; we are told in another of the Jaina sacred books, the A'cārāṅga Sutra, that " they observed, blamed, repented, confessed and did penance according to their sins, " and

* S. B. E. xxii. 250. † S. B. E. xxii. p. 251.
‡ S. B. E. xxii. p. 249. § S. B. E. xxii. 250.

finally attained a meritorious death by suicide*: "[reclining] on a bed of kus'a grass they rejected all food, and their bodies dried up by the last mortification of the flesh, which is to end in death." †

Mahāvira was now thirty, and with the permission of his elder brother, Nandivardhana, he resolved to enter upon the spiritual career which in India as in Europe has so often proved a fitting sphere for younger sons.

Dr. Hoernle ‡ tells us that the Nāta clan kept up a monastic establishment for monks of Pārsvanātha's order in Kollāga, and it was naturally this establishment that Mahāvira first joined. But their rule did not seem to him stringent enough, and after a year and a month he separated from them on the question of wearing clothes, § and "after that time walked about naked and accepted alms in the hollow of his hand." The question of wearing clothes or not was destined to become a crucial one in the history of Jainism, for it was on this point that its two great sects divided.

It is difficult to understand why Mahāvira laid such great stress on nudity. Sir Monier Williams ¶ gives what is at least a possible explanation. "The Jains," he says, "like all other ascetics, were impressed with the idea that it was necessary to maintain a defensive warfare against the assault of evil passions, by keeping under the body and

* A way of gaining merit still practised among the Jaina.

† S. B. E. xxii. 194.

‡ Annual Address, A. S. B., 1898.

§ A Jaina tradition says that Mahāvira on joining the order had only retained one cloth given to him by the god Indra.

¶ Buddhism. p. 530.

subduing it. They had also a notion that a sense of shame implied sin, so that if there were no sin in the world there would be no shame. Hence they argued rather illogically that to get rid of clothes was to get rid of sin; and every ascetic who aimed at sinlessness was enjoined to walk about naked, with the air or sky (Dig) as his sole covering." For twelve years Mahāvira wandered naked and homeless over the land, never resting during summer or winter for more than a single night in a village or for more than five nights in a town,* begging his food and indifferent whether good or bad were given to him, guarding his thoughts, guarding his words, guarding his senses, his heart as pure as water in autumn, and himself as unsoiled as the leaf of a lotus.

At last in the thirteenth year he reached enlightenment. He was sitting under a s'āl tree on the banks of a river not far from the town of Grimbhikagrāma, in the position† that is now so familiar from Buddhist statues, with legs and arms crossed. He had fasted for two days and a half, exposed to the heat of the sun without even drinking water, when, "engaged in deep meditation, he reached the highest knowledge and intuition, called Kevala, which is infinite, supreme, unobstructed, unimpeded, complete and full."‡ He had now become a Jina (*i. e.* Victor), an Arihanta (*i. e.*

---

* S. B. E. xxii. 260, ff. (Rules still binding on Jaina monks and nuns, though they have enlarged the one night into a week and the five nights into a month.)

† A popular Jaina tradition declares that at the time of receiving enlightenment Mahāvira was sitting in the *godoha āsana* posture (*i. e.* the position of milking a cow.)

‡ S. B. E. xxii. 263.

Venerable One), a Kevali (*i. e.* Possessor of *Kevala* [केवल] or spiritual nature) and a Mahāvira (or Great Hero), and by each of this galaxy of titles he is varyingly called. Now "he knew and saw all conditions of the world, of gods, of men and demons; whence they come, whither they go, whether they are born as men or animals or become gods or hell-beings, the ideas, the thoughts of their minds, the food, doings, desires, the open and secret deeds of all the living beings in the whole world" *

It is from his title of Jina that his sect and system derive their name. The Buddhist name for Mahāvira, however, is Nātaputta, from his clan, and the Jaina scriptures occasionally call him Vesāliya from his birth place.

For thirty years more Mahāvira taught his doctrine, gathering followers round him. Gos'āla had been his first disciple. Jacobi † thinks he was the head of an independent sect, who threw in his lot for a time with Mahāvira but separated on the question of leadership, but Dr. Hoernle ‡ believes him to have been a follower who after six years quarrelled with his master and became head of the A'jivika order of monks, which are mentioned on As'oka's pillar, about 234 B. C., but which have long ceased to exist. In the Sutrakṛitāṅga § a dispute between Gos'āla and a zealous disciple of Mahāvira is recorded, in which of course Gos'āla is ignominiously routed. This Gos'āla must have been a cantankerous fellow, for he is mentioned in the Buddhist Scriptures as an antagonist of Buddha also.

Mahāvira made many converts to his religious system

---

* S. B. E. xxii. 263. † S. B. E. xlv. Introd: p. xxix.

‡ Annual Address, A. S. B. 1898 p. 41. § S. B. E. xlv. 409.

and organised an order of ascetics in the lands under the sway of his royal kinsfolk, in Srāvasti, Videha, Magadha and Aṅga (the modern Oudh and the provinces of Tirhut and Bihār),* the very countries traversed by his great rival Buddha. During the rainy seasons he would cease from his peregrinations, lest he should injure any of the abundant life then springing into being, staying for four months in some town. Twelve rainy seasons he passed thus in his own town of Vais'āli.

He gained eleven disciples who remained true to him, and they in turn instructed 4,200 monks.

His great disciple Sudharmā survived him; it is through him that Jainism itself has been preserved, and he hands down in the Sutrakṛitāṅga many of the discourses of his master.

The Kalpa Sutra records with curious iteration the death of Mahāvira in his seventy second year. He spent his last rainy season in the town of Pāpāpuri (probably the modern Padraona, as General Sir A. Cunningham thinks,) and at the time of early morning, in king Hastipāla's Office of the Writers, sitting in the Samparyaṅka posture and reciting the fifty five lectures which detail the results of Karma, he "died, went off, quitted the world, cut asunder the ties of birth, old age and death; became a Siddha, a Buddha, a Mukta, a maker of the end to all misery." †

Mahāvira must have been a man of strong personality to have done the work he did amongst his warrior kinsfolk; but he never seems to have had the same personal magnetism

* Bühler, Indian Sect of the Jainas. p. 27.

† S. B. E. xxii. 264.

which is associated with the name of Buddha. That he was possessed of great powers of persuasion and organisation is shewn by his having brought over the order of Pārs'vanātha (to which he had originally belonged) to his later views, and having prevented anything like a split in his life time. Dr. Hopkins records the tradition that he died in a fit of apoplectic rage, a story scarcely credible of a man whose whole life had been so disciplined and controlled, that "he was indifferent alike to the smell of ordure and of sandal, to straw and jewels, dirt and gold, pleasure and pain, attached neither to this world nor to that beyond, desiring neither life nor death."* Indeed it is almost pathetic to think of a man, originally possessed of so full and vivid a personality, having so docked his life of all feeling as to leave no conceivable room for any cause which could excite "apoplectic rage." That in spite of everything he remained loveable is shewn by the story of his oldest disciple, Indrabhuti, who had cut himself off from every tie that held him back from Kevala except one, his love for his master, and not till the night Mahāvira died was he able to cut asunder this last tie and attain the highest knowledge.†

The story of Mahāvira is followed in the Kalpa Sutra by that of an earlier saint, Pārs'va (or Pārs'vanātha), who seems to have been an historical personage and the founder of the order of the Nirgrantha which Mahāvira won over.‡

Mahāvira is counted as the twenty-fourth Tirthaṅkara [*Sanskrit* Tirthakara (तीर्थकर), *Gujarāti* Tirthaṅkara (તીર્થંકર)],

* S. B. E. xxii. 262.

† S. B. E. xxii. 265.

‡ Indeed the name of Nirgrantha (one without ties) soon attached itself to the followers of Mahāvira and is that by which the Jaina were in early times known. See Hoernle, A. S. B., 1898, p. 42.

or ford maker who has crossed the troubled river of constant births or transmigration (Saṁsāra [સંસાર]) to the haven of Liberation; Pārs'va is the twenty-third, and behind him stretch the other Tirthaṅkara, whose length of life and height of stature grow ever greater and greater as they recede further and further into the mists of tradition. We shall return to them later when we are discussing Jaina beliefs.

RISE OF THE JAINA SECTS.

The history of Jainism subsequent to the death of Mahāvira is not marked by many outstanding events, excepting the great schism which divided the order into the white clothed Svetāmbara and the nude or "sky clothed" Digambara. A great famine arose in 310 B. C., some two centuries after the death of Mahāvira, in Magadha (Bihār), and, as sometimes happens in India at the present day, under pressure of the famine a great part of the population emigrated, amongst them Bhadrabāhu, the then head of the Jaina community, and a number of his people. These went to Southern India, and a certain Sthulabhadra assumed the leadership of those left behind in Magadha.

Svetambara and Digambara.

This Sthulabhadra was evidently an energetic worker, and under his rule a great council was held at Pātaliputra (Patna), which amongst other things collected the Jaina sacred books.

At this time also the home keeping Jaina adopted some sort of dress, and when the famine was over and the exiles returned, they found that their weaker brethren had not only lacked the strength of character to leave their own land but also the moral courage to keep their rule.

The orthodox Digambara Jaina refused to have any fellowship with their clothed (Svetāmbara) brethren, and thus laid a foundation for the schism which definitely arose in 82 A. D. and has lasted to this day. It seems probable that two parties in the community had always existed, and that only distance had been needed to enable the divergence to develop.

The Digambara refuse to acknowledge the work of the Council of Pātaliputra and say that the original sacred books have been lost.

The manuscripts authorized by the first council eventually grew scarce and fell into disorder, and so a second great council was held at Vallabhi, in Gujarat, under the presidency of Devarddhi, the head of one of the schools, which revised them and thus fixed the Svetāmbara canon of the scriptures.

This, briefly, is the account given by Dr. Hoernle* of the historic Jaina tradition of their own history and sacred books, and he goes on to show how in 1896 most striking corroboration of the early date of the great schism was found by Prof. Bühler when deciphering the inscriptions in Madura.

The modern Jaina tradition however in Western India differs slightly from this account, and I am indebted to a learned Jaina gentleman for the following particulars.

He agrees with Dr. Hoernle as to the cause of the complete divergence between the Svetāmbara and Digambara sects, and holds that under Mahāvira there had been two sections, the *Jinakalpi* (જીનકલ્પી), who were very rigid in their observance of the rule, and the *Sthivarakalpi* (સ્થિવરકલ્પી), who owing to old age or illness were allowed to relax the rule so far as to wear clothes and to eat delicacies.

The Svetāmbara canon was not committed to writing† for 980 years after the death of Mahāvira, then, under the

* Annual Address, A. S. B. 1898. p. 47 ff.

† A Jaina *Sādhu* has kindly supplied me with the following legend as to the cause of the Svetāmbara scriptures being committed to

presidency of Devarddhi Kṣamās'ramaṇa, forty-five *Shāstras* were written down, which took thirteen years to accomplish. The Svetāmbara believe that originally there had been eighty four scriptures but that thirty nine had been lost.

The remaining forty five were first written and published in Valā (Gohelvāḍ Prānt,) Kāṭhiāvāḍ. All the sects believe that at this time certain of Mahāvira's precepts which were no longer suited to society were omitted.

The Scriptures were written in Arddha Māgadhi, commentaries on them have been written in Sanskrit, and there are also Gujarāti translations of the text. The Svetāmbara do not allow laymen or women to read their Scriptures; these may only read certain small books of extracts which have been made from them.

Monks are allowed to read the Sacred books, and so are nuns, though it is very unusual for the latter to be sufficiently educated to be able to do so.

Dhundhia or Sthanakavasi.

There is however a branch of the Svetāmbara Jaina who permit the laity to read their Sacred books. These are the *Dhunḍhiā* (ઢુંઢીઆ) or, as they prefer to be called, the *Sthānakavāsi* (સ્થાનકવાસી) Jaina. They give the following account of their origin. About five hundred years ago

---

writing. A certain monk was ill and needed ginger as a remedy for his sickness. By their rule the monks were allowed to beg for any necessary medicine, but the unused portion must be returned by night fall. The monks failed to return the unused ginger, and when their *guru* saw how forgetful they had become, he felt it was no longer safe to trust the Scriptures to their memories.

in Ahmedabad a certain Svetāmbara Jaina* was asked to copy certain sacred Svetāmbara books, and whilst making the close study of them necessary for the work, he realized that there was no mention of idolatry in them. He eventually founded a reformed and non-idolatrous sect† which rejects any of the Svetāmbara Scriptures that treat of idols or idol worship, and allows the common people to read the books it has retained.

The Digambara Canon.

The Digambara reject the Svetāmbara Canon. They have formed their own Scriptures, Purāna and Grantha, containing lives of the Tirthaṅkara and of great monks and certain rules of conduct, as well as some mathematics, science and philosophy. These scriptures are specially noted for their philosophy, though like the Svetāmbara Sacred Books, on which indeed they are based, they treat of idol worship also. They (like the Dhuṇḍhiā Scriptures) are open to the laity.

Treasure Houses.

There are famous Treasure Houses of the Jaina Scriptures at Pātan (near Siddhpur), Cambay and Jesalmir (in Rajputana), and there is a smaller one at Limbaḍi (in Kāṭhiāvāḍ).

They are connected with Jaina monasteries, but can scarcely be called Libraries, for it is very difficult for even Jaina to gain access to them, and practically impossible for a non-Jaina.

* The Dhundhiā say the copyist's name was Lonkā. Mr. Bhimbhāi Kirpārām says the reformer was a priest of the Lonkā sect who rebelled against the authority of his Shripujya and was expelled. Bombay Gazetteer. Vol. ix. Part i. p. 106.

† They are also known in Mālwā as Sādhumārgi (સાધુમાર્ગી) Jaina.

THE JAINA SCRIPTURES.

The following is the Canon of Scriptures held by the Jaina of Western India, together with brief notes as to their contents. Various sects and sub-sects differ very much with regard to the Chedagrantha, Muḷagrantha and Payannā, but all Svetāmbara and Sthānakavāsi practically agree with regard to the Aṅga and Upāṅga. They hold that originally there were Twelve Aṅga, but that one, the Dṛis'tivāda Aṅga (દ્રિષ્ટિવાદ અંગ) containing an account of the fourteen Purva or Sciences, was destroyed.

A. The Eleven Anga (અંગ).

1. *The A'cārāṅga Sutra* (આચારાંગ સૂત્ર). A book of rules for monks and recluses, together with the life of Mahāvira.

2. *The Suyagaḍāṅga Sutra* (સૂયગડાંગ સૂત્ર), which contains a description of the faiths which prevailed at the time when Jainism arose, and which deals also with tranquility of mind and with the knowledge that destroys our attachment to the world.

3. *The Thāṇāṅga Sutra* (ઠાણાંગ સૂત્ર). A book concerned with the numbers in which things exist. Thus, under the heading "*one*" are grouped all things which exist singly as soul; similarly under "*two*" are mentioned all things of which there are pairs, as Love and Hatred; under "*three*" Birth, Life and Death; under "*four*" Anger, Pride, Deceit, Avarice.

4. *The Samavāyāṅga Sutra* (સમવાયાંગ સૂત્ર). This book contains various comparisons of opposites, as the

power that moves bodies and the power that keeps them stationary; the comparison being made with regard to substance, space, time, and emotion.

5. *Bhagavatiji* (ભગવતીજી) or *Vivihāpannanti* (વિવિહાપન્નત્તિ). This is the great Sutra and is held in the highest honour. It contains the questions which Gautama asked Mahāvira and the latter's answers. It deals chiefly with religious philosophy.

6. *Jñātādharma Kathāṅga* (જ્ઞાતાધર્મ કથાંગ) contains moral stories about Faith, Knowledge and Soul; e. g. Two men were each given a peahen's egg. One man, being faithless, was for ever shaking his egg whilst it was hatching, to see how it was progressing, and so destroyed the chicken, but the believing man, who quietly left his egg alone till the appointed time, was rewarded with a beautiful peacock.

7. *Upāsaka Das'āṅga* (ઉપાસક દશાંગ) contains the biographies of ten eminent laymen and the eleven steps a layman should take to attain Liberation (Mokṣa).

8. *Antagaḍa Das'āṅga* (અન્તગડ દશાંગ). The lives of ten Preceptors (*A'cārya* [આચાર્ય]), who possessed the greatest powers of endurance, were freed from the eight Karma and attained Mokṣa in the same life, together with the lives of some other Kevali.

9. *Anuttarovavāi Das'āṅga* (અનુત્તરોવવાઇ દશાંગ). The lives of ten Preceptors who attained to Anuttaravimāna (અનુત્તરવિમાન), i. e. one stage short of Mokṣa, in the same life.

10. *Pras'na Vyākaraṇa* (પ્રશ્ન વ્યાકરણ) deals chiefly with the path of Karma and its destruction.

11. *Vipāka Sutra* (વિપાક સૂત્ર) describes the enjoyment of the fruit of good actions and the suffering entailed by evil deeds.

B Twelve Upanga (ઉપાંગ).

1. *Uvavāi* (ઉવવાઇ) gives more details of the various ceremonies and places alluded to in the Aṅga.

2. *Rāyapaseṇi* (રાયપસેણી) contains the various questions asked by King Parades'i and the answers given by the Sage Kes'i.

3. *Jivābhigama* (જીવાભિગમ). In this is given a full account of the soul and all that appertains to it, together with various other details concerning the Jaina faith.

4. *Pannavaṇā* (પન્નવણા). This, too, deals with the soul, and also with matter.

5. *Jambudivapannati* (જંબુદ્વીપપન્નતિ) contains the geography of the island of Jambu (which many believe to be Modern Asia), its seven divisions, mountains, rivers, etc.

6. *Candapannati* (ચંદપન્નતિ) } both deal with astronomy and astrology.
7. *Surapannati* (સુરપન્નતિ) }

8. *Nirāvaliā** (નિરાવલીઆ). A description of Hell and of the men who have gone there, including the ten Kālikumāra (ten bad princes who committed many murders).

9. *Kappavadis'ayyā* (કપ્પવડીશય્યા). A description of the Kalpa, or lower division of Heaven, and a short account of those who have gone there.

---

* The ગીરનાર માહાત્મ્ય p. 187 gives કપ્પિઆ (Kappiā) instead of Nirāvaliā.

10. *Pupphiyā* (પુપ્ફિયા). An account of the heavens and different planets, and of the celestial cars which convey people from the earth to the planets, together with a description of the people who are entitled to enter heaven.

11. *Puphachuliā* (પુફચુલીઆ). An account of the nun " Puphachulā " (પુફચુલા), her virtues and her disciples.

12. *Vanhidas'ā* (વન્હિદશા). An account of the great men who were born in the Vishnu family; how they conquered Dwārkā, obtained initiation, maintained self control and attained Mokṣa. It is interesting to note that according to Jaina belief Krishna was a Jaina, a cousin of Neminātha, the twenty-second Tirthaṅkara, and that he will himself in his next Incarnation be one of their new Twenty-four Tirthaṅkara.

C. **Six Chedagrantha** (છેદગ્રંથ). (Books partially destroyed, or books teaching how to destroy sin.)

1. *Vyavahāra Sutra* (વ્યવહાર સુત્ર).
2. *Bṛihatkalpa* (બૃહત્કલ્પ).
3. *Das'ās'rutaskandha* (દશાશ્રુતસ્કંધ).
4. *Nis'itha* (નિશિથ).

These four books all contain rules which monks and nuns must observe as to the taking of food, water, clothes, pots, etc., and the penalties to be undergone for violating any of these regulations.

As we have already seen, the Svetāmbara hardly ever allow their books to be read by laymen, and although the Sthānakavāsi do not thus restrict the use of the scriptures, even they do not like the laity to see these four books, which, they say, are meant for monks only.

The remaining two Chedagrantha are not recognised by Sthānakavāsi but only by Svetāmbara Jaina. Their names are:—

5. *Mahānis'itha* (મહાનિશિથ).

6. *Jitakalpa* (જીતકલ્પ).

D. Four Mulagrantha (મુળગ્રંથ), (according to the Svetāmbara canon.)

1. *Das'avaikālika* (દશવૈકાલિક). An epitome of the rules for monks with regard to the division of their time.

2. *Uttarādhyayana* (ઉત્તરાધ્યયન). A very famous and important book, containing the lives of eminent saints, and teaching that a man is raised by his Karma and not his birth. It deals too with celibacy, discipline and character, and also records the advice given by Mahāvira to his disciples two days before he entered Mokṣa. Its last chapters are devoted to an important and lengthy discussion on Soul and Matter.

3. *A'vas'yaka* (આવશ્યક). The morning and evening duties of Jaina, (Paḍikamaṇuṁ, etc.) Various sects of Svetāmbara have different versions of this book, and whereas versions of other scriptures in use among different sects are much alike, the versions of this one differ widely from each other.

4. *Oghaniryukti* (ઓઘનિર્યુક્તિ). This is on similar lines, but is not accepted by the Sthānakavāsi.

Of these four the Sthānakavāsi accept only the first two as Muḷagrantha and consider the A'vas'yaka to be not a Muḷagrantha but the last of all the scriptures.

Four Mulagrantha, (according to the Sthānakavāsī Canon.)

1. *Das'avāikālika* દશવૈકાલિક.
2. *Uttarādhyayana* ઉત્તરાધ્યયન.
3. *Nandi Sutra* (નન્દી સૂત્ર.) A history of the eighty-four original scriptures and their destruction, and also of the saints who succeeded Mahāvira.
4. *Anuyogadvāra* (અનુયેાગદ્વાર.) A book on logic.

The Svetāmbara and Sthānakavāsi alike believe that their religion is decaying, and that their scriptures are being destroyed; they think however that the Four Muḷagrantha will be the last to perish.

This completes the list of the thirty-two scriptures accepted by the Sthānakavāsi.

In addition the Svetāmbara accept the following:—

E Ten Payanna (પયન્ના) or Miscellaneous Books.

1. *Causarana* (ચઉસરણ,) in which people are exhorted to seek the protection of—

Arihanta (અરિહંત)
Siddha (સિદ્ધ)
Sādhu (સાધુ)
Dharma (ધર્મ) *i. e.* (the Jaina) Religion.

2. *Santhārā Payannā* (સંથારા પયન્ના). Another book of good advice, which urges people to fulfil all their vows during their life time, to confess their sins, and to die peacefully without any desire for longer life.

3. *Tandulavsyāliā* (તંદુલવેયાલીઆ,) telling of the nourishment and dangers of the embryo in the womb.

4. *Candāvijaya* (ચંદાવિજય) contains stories about the moon, its eclipse, distance from the earth, etc., needless to say not in accordance with Western Science.

5. *Ganivijaya* (ગણિવિજય.) A book of arithmetic.

6. *Devindathuo* (દેવિંદથુઓ.) Songs in praise of Indra, the highest of the gods inhabiting *swarga*. (Some, however, hold that these are really songs sung by Indra in praise of the *Siddha*).

7. *Virathuo* (વીરથુઓ.) Songs in praise of Mahāvira.

8. *Gacchācāra* (ગચ્છાચાર) gives rules of conduct binding on the members of different Jaina sects.

9. *Jyotikaraṇḍa* (જ્યોતિકરંડ.) A book of astrology, dreams, omens, etc.

10. *A'yuḥpaccakhāṇa* (આયુઃપચ્ચખાણ.) A book of the vows which a man should take at the time of his death in the presence of a monk or nun. As these are considered too difficult for any one to perform, he is allowed in case of recovery to keep them in a modified form, and to permit of this he may take them in either a limited (મર્યાદિત) or unlimited (અમર્યાદિત) form: e. g. he vows in the limited form not to lie; if on his recovery he should, nevertheless, tell a lie in the course of his daily business, he would be held to have committed the sin of lying but not that of vow breaking.

The Digambara Scriptures.

The following is the list of Digambara Scriptures given by Dr. Burgess.*

---

* Digambara Jaina Iconography. p. 1.

1. *Prathamānuyoga* (પ્રથમાનુયોગ) which contains all works on legends and history, including the twenty four Purāṇa with the lives of the Tirthaṅkara.

2. *Karaṇānuyoga* (કરણાનુયોગ) which includes all their books dealing with Cosmogony.

3. *Dravyānuyoga* (દ્રવ્યાનુયોગ) or books treating of doctrine and philosophy.

4. *Caraṇānuyoga* (ચરણાનુયોગ) in which *āchāra* customs, worship etc. are described.

JAINA ASCETICS.

The Jaina say that one of Mahāvira's great messages to the human race was that man could attain salvation through his own efforts independently of Brahmanic aid. Unlike Buddha, he laid the greatest stress on asceticism as a means towards attaining that end, and Jainism has proved the forerunner of much of the most revolting asceticism current in the India of today. It has been said that as knowledge is wisdom to the Brahman, and purity and love to the Buddhist, so is asceticism wisdom to the Jaina.

Monks.

It is easier for an ascetic or Yati (યતિ) to attain heaven than for a layman, but before a man may become an ascetic he must obtain leave from his parents or guardians. If he be married he may still become a Yati (or Sādhu) on gaining his wife's permission or after her death, but a Bāla brahmacāri (બાલ બ્રહ્મચારી), *i. e.* a man who has never been married, is held in higher honour.

Before his initiation or dikṣā (દીક્ષા) the Yati gives up everything save five garments (three upper and two lower

Possessions.

ones), and a blanket; in the case of a Svetāmbara these would be yellow in colour, and in that of a Sthānakavāsi white; the Digambara, of course, keeps no clothing. (In Ahmedabad some of the Svetāmbara ascetics wear white with yellow over it, and these men are considered to be more devout).

He keeps also two or three more pieces of cloth to wrap round his food and to strain his drinking water, and a piece of cloth to wear over his mouth. A Sthānakavāsi sādhu must keep his mouth covered night and day, so he wears this mouth cloth or *mumati* (મુમતી)* tied on with strings, and when lay people talk to Sthānakavāsi ascetics they must cover their mouths. It is sufficient for the Svetāmbara sādhus to keep their mouth cloth in their hands.

Besides his cloth the monk generally has a long rod, which must not be hollow lest it should entrap and kill an insect, and a brush (Rajoṇo રજોહરણો), which is used to protect insects by sweeping them out of danger. Its whisk is of wool, and the Sthānakavāsi, who sweep more carefully than the Svetāmbara, have a bigger brush with a longer handle. The Digambara Sādhu who live in the jungle frequently use a peacock's feather instead of a brush.

The ascetic is allowed to possess five pots, which must be gourds, or else fashioned from wood. Brass vessels are not permitted, as a sādhu must possess no metal; thus if he borrow a needle he must return it by sunset, lest the sin of covetousness should grow upon him, and if he is obliged to wear spectacles they must be framed in wood. He is also allowed to keep a wooden jug.

These are henceforth to be his sole possessions, and when they grow old he must not ask for new ones, but must wait till they are given to him.† A woman wishing to become a nun must give up all her property in the same way, excepting that she is allowed to keep two additional garments.

---

* Also called muhapati (મુહપતી) or mukhapaṭṭikā (મુખપટ્ટિકા).

† Even then the donor may not bring them to him at the Upāsaro, but inviting him to his house must say as he offers them that they are more than he requires for his own use.

Initiation.

At the time of his initiation the man is led in procession through the city with much pomp and ceremony to a banyan tree.

Next comes the removal of the hair, which is performed outside the city in some room or tent. The candidate's head is shaved all over, with the exception of one small lock of hair which is pulled out under a tree. After six months the ascetic will have to get rid of his hair again, but this time it must all be pulled out, the merciful aid of partial shaving being only given the first time.

This hair plucking is a rite peculiar to the Jaina and is looked on by them as of great importance; it is always done in preparation for the yearly Pajjusaṇa, as well as at other times if necessary.

A mixture of ashes etc. is applied to his head, and the following mantra is whispered in his ear :—

करेमि भंते सामायं सावजजोगं पचखामि. जावजिवाए पज्जुवासामि. (दुविहं तिविहेणं न करोमि न कारवेमि) मणसा वयसा कायसा तस्सभंते पडिकमाभि निंदामि गरिहामि अप्पाणं वोसिरामि।

The bracketed words are sometimes changed and the following words substituted for them :—

तिविहं तिविहेणं न करोमि न कारवोमि, करंत नाणु जाणइ।

In the first case he promises not to infringe his vows by any of the three Daṇḍa, (દંડ) *i. e.* mind, speech, or action, nor to cause any one else to do so; in the second case he further promises not to share in the result of any one having done so.

If the ascetic be a Digambara or Svetāmbara, he will take a new name; if he be a Sthānakavāsi, however, he will still retain his old one.

The Svetāmbara call male ascetics Saṁvegi (સંવેગી) and the nuns Garaṇiji (ગરણીજી), the Sthānakavāsi call the men Mahāpuruṣa (મહાપુરૂષ) or Pujya (પૂજ્ય) and the women Mahāsati (મહાસતી) or A'rajā (આરજા).

Nuns.

The initiation ceremony for a nun is practically the same as for a monk, excepting that the *mantra* is whispered into her ear by a Sādhvi (female ascetic) instead of a Sādhu. Her head too is shaved for the first time, but afterwards when the hair grows it is pulled out hair by hair. This is done about twice a year by one nun for another, and is called *Loca* (લોચ).* If a woman wishes to become a nun she may do so, but she must first obtain her husband's consent, or, if unmarried or widowed, the consent of her parents or guardians.

In any case she must be well instructed in the tenets of the Jaina faith before she can be "professed," and the instruction should last from six months to two years. At any time before her "profession" she can go back into the world, and some women seem to take the course of instruction without any intention of becoming nuns.

Daily Life of a Novice.

A woman who had not yet been professed most kindly gave me the following account of her day's routine. About 5 A. M. she rose, and in her own house before sunrise she made confession of the night's sin (Rāyasi Paḍikamaṇuṁ રાયસી પડીકમણું). At sunrise she went to the nuns' house or

* When I asked a nun if this did not hurt very much she replied: "Hurt? Of course it does, but what's that compared with the bother and worry of a husband" ! !

Upāsaro (ઉપાસરો), and listened for an hour to the reading of the scriptures or a sermon by a nun. From eight to twelve she was busied with the work of her own house, but at two o'clock, after her midday rest, she went back to the Upāsaro for meditation (Sāmāyika સામાયિક). She had to be home again to take her daily meal before sunset, and after sunset she made her confession of the day's sin (Devasi Paḍikamaṇuṁ દેવસી પડીક્રમણું). Twice during the day she did palewaṇa (પલેવણ), *i. e.* searched her clothing to find if there were any insects in it, and, if she found any, removed them carefully that they might take no injury.

Daily Life of a Nun.

After she should become a nun, she would have the same duty of morning confession and listening to the scriptures. In addition, not having any household duties, she would study till nine A. M., and then go out and beg for water. (The only water an ascetic can take must have been boiled to destroy any life in it, and boiled moreover not more than four hours previously, lest new life be formed in it.) She would also have to go and beg for food at eleven o'clock, and again at five in the evening, and must arrange never to have any food left over at night, lest insect life should form in it. Strictly speaking, she should only eat once and only sleep for three hours during the twenty-four. During the night she should if possible rise and pray twice. In many places however these rules have fallen into disuse.

The life of a nun is an arduous one, for she must live the same wandering life as a monk, though always accompanied by a female companion. She is however held in the greatest honour, as is shewn in the respect paid to her at her death.

The Funeral of an Araja

By the courtesy of some Sthānakavāsī nuns I was allowed to be present at the funeral of one of their number.

When the moment of death approached, devout laywomen were called in to attend on the dying nun, whom they placed in the sitting (or Kāusagga) posture on one of the wooden bedsteads in the Upāsaro; the other nuns withdrew to another part of the room, where they sat repeating certain *Mantras*, taking no part in the funeral rites, though they were obliged to fast till all was completed. As soon as the nun died, the laywomen tied her to a short plank to keep her in the sitting posture, and wrapped a rich cloth of gold brocade over her body, still wearing its nun's robes of simple white and its *mumati* or mouth covering.

In the mean time a costly palanquin of teak wood had been prepared, the top of which resembled a temple, with numerous pinnacles each bearing a flag, while the inside was lined with exquisite silk and rich cushions.

The body was carried from the Upāsaro to the palanquin by laymen, who removed the plank and tied the corpse, still in the sitting posture, to some supports at the back and arranged the cushions round it.

A procession was then formed to the river bank; it was headed by a royal horse and drum lent by the ruler of the State, after which came men seated in a cart beating religious drums, followed by people on foot playing on ordinary drums and musical instruments.

The boys from the Jaina schools furnished a guard of honour; some bore silver sticks and banners on which were written: જય જિનેંદ્ર Jaya Jinendra! (Victory to the Highest of the Jina), whilst others sang Jaina songs about the transitoriness of life.

After these came a cart containing the sandal wood, cocoanuts and tins of clarified butter necessary for the funeral rites, together with a bag of Juvāra (જુવાર), a kind of millet, which would be distributed to the poor when the body was burnt.

Hindu, not as one would have expected Jaina, ascetics followed, playing cymbals and other musical instruments, and owing to the friendliness that exists in Kāthiāwāḍ between the sects, both Svetāmbara and Sthānakavāsi laymen followed the ascetics. (I was assured that in most places the Svetāmbara would not have paid such honour to a nun of another sect).

These were succeeded by people scattering money, food and flowers amongst the crowd of onlookers. There was a great rush amongst the spectators to try and get hold of these, as they are supposed to have the power of fulfilling wishes.

The palanquin itself came next, and this had to be guarded by police, as any woman who can tear a piece of a dead nun's dress thinks she has secured an infallible charm against childlessness.

A dozen or more men carried the palanquin, and there are always eager volunteers for the post of bearer, which is considered very meritorious. Those who cannot act as bearers are given lighted sticks of incense and follow the palanquin with the crowd through the city to the burning ghāt shouting "jaya jinendra."

At the ghāt the funeral pyre was built, its lowest layer of the wood of the *pipal* tree; on this sandal wood was arranged with cocoanuts on the top. On the pyre they placed the palanquin and its burden, and over both were scattered pieces of cotton wool dipped in clarified butter. A dozen men set fire to the palanquin in different places, the scattered cotton wool making it ignite quickly.

By the end of four hours the pyre was completely consumed, and the Jaina, leaving the ashes on the river bank, bathed, and donning the fresh clothes that had been brought to them from their homes, returned in a body to the men's Upāsaro, where they had to listen to a sermon and then to sit in the Kāusagga posture and meditate. When this was over they went to the women's Upāsaro, where the laywomen (who could not go to the ghāt) and the nuns had been sitting all day meditating and listening to sermons; to these they offered their condolences, and then had to listen to yet another sermon on the transitoriness of life before seeking their homes. It was curious to notice that, though Hindu ascetics had taken part in the procession, no Jaina ascetics, male or female, were permitted to do so. The cost of this nun's funeral was about five hundred rupees, the palanquin alone costing two hundred. During the whole day business throughout the city was practically at a stand still, all the grain and vegetable markets and most of the other shops being closed.

Five Great Vows or Pancha Mahavrata.

Every ascetic must take the five great vows (પાંચ મહાવ્રત) which Mahāvira ordained. These vows, it will be noticed, resemble the Buddhist vows, but still more the ancient

Brahmanic vows on which they are doubtless both founded.*

The first vow the Jaina ascetic takes is to refrain from destroying life, and runs as follows:—"I renounce all killing of living beings, whether subtile or gross, whether movable or immovable. Nor shall I myself kill living beings (nor cause others to do it, nor consent to it). As long as I live, I confess and blame, repent and exempt myself of these sins, in the thrice threefold way, in mind, speech and body." †

1. Ahimsa Vrata
અહિંસા વ્રત.

This (which is also the first vow taken by the Brahman and Buddhist ascetics) the Jaina sect divide into nine, and so make it cover an immense field. They are not to kill in word, thought or deed; they are not to cause any one to kill in word, thought or deed; they are not to support any one who kills in word, thought or deed. This vow, on which the Jaina lay the greatest stress, they regularly break. They are most careful not to destroy life themselves, but are quite willing to "consent" to others doing it and to reap the benefit. An ascetic for instance may not take water that has not been boiled, lest it contain life, neither may he boil it; but by taking water that another has boiled he certainly "consents" to their action in boiling it. It has been suggested that the real reason for the vow was not so much unselfish kindness to animals as the selfish fear of being haunted by the spirit of the dead.‡

* For the comparison of Jainism with Buddhism generally see Jacobi's Introduction to the Jaina Sutras, S. B. E. xxii. pp. xix ff.

† Acārānga Sutra. S. B. E. Vol. xxii. p. 202.

‡ Cp. Bombay Gazetteer. Vol. ix. Part i. p. 99.

2. Asatya Tyaga અસત્ય ત્યાગ.

The second great vow of the Jaina, the renouncing of all untruthfulness, runs thus:—"I renounce all vices of lying speech (arising) from anger or greed or fear or mirth. I shall neither myself speak lies, nor cause others to speak lies, nor consent to the speaking of lies by others. I confess and blame, repent and exempt myself of these sins in the thrice three-fold way, in mind, speech, and body." *

It is interesting to notice that, with regard to the order of the vows, the Jaina have here kept closer to the second Brahmanic vow of truthfulness than have the Buddhists, whose second vow is against stealing.

The Jaina carefully subdivide this vow, also, into nine.

3. Asteya Vrata અસ્તેય વ્રત.

The third vow runs:—"I renounce all taking of anything not given, either in a village or a town or a wood, either of little or much, of small or great, of living or lifeless things. I shall neither take myself what is not given, nor cause others to take it, nor consent to their taking it." † This vow is the third vow of the Brāhman ascetics, but the second of the Buddhists.

The Jaina subdivide this vow also in nine ways, and under it forbid a *guru* to take any child as a disciple without the leave of his parents, and insist on the ascetics dividing with each other the alms they have received. By it, too, an ascetic is forbidden to ask any individual for a house to live in without the consent of the principal laymen of the place. Once a man has given a house, he may never again be asked for alms.

---

* S. B. E. xxii. 204. † S. B. E. xxii. 205.

4. Brahmacarya Vrata બ્રહ્મચર્ય વ્રત

The fourth vow of the Jaina and Brāhman ascetics relates to chastity, which with Buddhist ascetics is the fifth vow.

The Jaina vow is as follows:—" I renounce all sexual pleasures, either with gods or men * * *. I shall not give way to sensuality." *

It has the usual nine subdivisions with regard to word, mind and deed, and by it, too, all Jaina are forbidden to drink wine, and ascetics are prohibited from eating highly seasoned dishes. †

5. Aparigraha Vrata અપરિગ્રહ વ્રત.

The fifth Jaina vow is the following:—" I renounce all attachments, whether little or much, small or great, living or lifeless; neither shall I myself form such attachments, nor cause others to do so, nor consent to their doing so." ‡ This vow forbids covetousness, and likes or dislikes in regard to such things as agreeable or disagreeable sounds, colours or smells.

The fifth vow with the Brāhman ascetic relates to liberality, and with the Buddhist to chastity. It will have been noticed how much more nearly the Jaina vows agree with those of the Brāhman than with those of the Buddhist ascetic.

6. Ra'tribhojana Tya'ga રાત્રીભોજન ત્યાગ.

The Svetāmbara add a sixth vow not to take a meal at night lest one should inadvertently take life. The Sthānakavāsi and Digambara say that this is included in the first vow of Ahiṁsā, under which one is expressly bound not to eat or drink without examining his food, lest he destroy life.

---

* S. B. E. xxii 207. † S. B. E. xxii 208. ‡ S. B. E. xxii 208.

Ten Duties of Monks or Nuns.

There are ten duties, the *Das'a Yatidharma* (દશ યતિધર્મ), binding on monks and nuns of all sects.

1. Ksama' ક્ષમા. An ascetic must bear and forgive any injury inflicted on him.

2. Nirlobhata' નિર્લોભતા. He must be absolutely free from greed. He must not covet new clothes even if in need of them, but must wait till they are offered to him, and even then he must only accept those of which the giver has no further need.

3. A'rjava આર્જવ. He must be perfectly straightforward and never be guilty of any kind of intrigue or fraud.

4. Ma'rdava માર્દવ. He must be absolutely humble, never proud of his purity of life, his learning, or any other virtue, and he must never speak a harsh word.

5. Tapa તપ. An ascetic must practise many austerities, which will all help to free him from rebirth.

These austerities are divided into Exterior and Interior.

(i) There are *Six Exterior Austerities.*

(a) Fasting (Anas'ana અનશન. *)* A monk must frequently fast, but the period for which he fasts may vary from one day to three months. During that time, besides water, he may only take the watery part of skimmed milk.

(b) Partial Fasting (Uṇodari ઉણોદરી). Instead of a total fast, an ascetic may vow to take only one-half or a third of his usual amount of food.

(c) *Restricting Diet (Vṛittisaṅkṣepa* વૃત્તિસંક્ષેપ). An ascetic may vow that for a period of time varying from one day to a month he will only eat five or six different articles of food, or he may vow to eat only one particular thing, failing to obtain which he will fast.

(d) *Abstaining from appetising food (Rasatyāga* રસત્યાગ). The ascetic promises to abstain from his favourite food (probably milk, ghi, or molasses) for a certain period.

(e) *Bodily austerities (Kāyakles'a* કાયક્લેશ). An ascetic torments his body in various ways, such as pulling out his hair, wearing insufficient clothing in winter and exposing his body to heat in summer.

(f) *The avoidance of all temptation (Saṁlinatā* સંલીનતા) is accounted another external austerity, and under this the cramping of limbs by sitting in uncomfortable postures is also included.

(ii) The following six austerities are *Interior.*

(a) *Expiation (Prāyas'cita* પ્રાયશ્ચિત). If the ascetic has committed any sin, he must confess it privately to his *guru* and perform the penance he imposes. Different kinds of penances are prescribed in the Scriptures for different offences. For example, if he has cast a stone (which the Jaina believes to possess one sense) into water (which also possesses one sense) he will be made to atone for the injury he has inflicted on sentient things by fasting or by extra Paḍikamaṇuṁ.

The greatest punishment the *guru* can inflict is to annul the ascetic's initiation and so "unfrock" him.

The *guru* is bound by the Scriptures to secresy with regard to Confession.

(b) The ascetic must also pay *Reverence* to his superiors (*Vinaya* વિનય). An ascetic who has no reverence for his superiors will never gain heaven.

(c) An ascetic must *serve* his superiors and the afflicted. This is called *Vaiyāvacca* વૈયાવચ્ચ. He must bring water and food for his *guru* and massage him when tired.

(d) Neither must an ascetic neglect the duty of *Study* (*Svādhyāya* સ્વાધ્યાય). He must gain knowledge by reading, by questioning, by remembering, by discussion, and by preaching.

(e) *Meditation* (*Dhyāna* ધ્યાન). There are two bad ways of meditation which a monk is bound to renounce, *i. e.* wailing for the dead, and remembering with anger any personal injuries he may have suffered. He is however bound to meditate in the good ways, by being absorbed in religious thought, and by being so freed from earthly thoughts as to be able to think of spiritual things.

(f) The last interior austerity which an ascetic must practise is absolute *Indifference* to his physical state (*Utsarga* ઉત્સર્ગ). In order to gain this indifference he sits in a particular position, which he must not change even if a serpent draw nigh!

The restraint of the passions is the sixth duty binding on all monks and nuns.

6. Saṁyama સંયમ.

The seventh duty is to be absolutely truthful in every particular. An ascetic must not tell any "white" or conventional lies, he must not speak ambiguously, his speech must be free from all egotism and simply consist of the plain unvarnished truth.

7. Satya સત્ય.

8. S'auca શૌચ. The eighth duty is purity.

9. A'kincinya આકિંચિન્ય. An ascetic must have no possessions.

10. Brahmacarya બ્રહ્મચર્ય. An ascetic must strictly observe celibacy.

It will be noticed that the last five duties closely resemble the five great vows.

Wandering life.

The A'cārāṅga Sutra says that he who is well provided with these great vows and their clauses is really houseless, and certainly the Jaina ascetic is Aṇagāra (અણગાર).

Both monk and nun must wander from village to village, begging as they go, and never staying at one place for any length of time. The old command was that they should stay only one night in a village and not more than five in a town, but this they now interpret as permission to stay for a week in a village and a month in a town. During the rainy season, however, they must stay in the same place for four months, lest they should injure any of the insect or plant life which is then so abundant. They must pass each rainy season at a different place, or must at least let three years elapse before they return to the same place.

Itinerancy.

The Svetāmbara, as a rule, only go to those villages where there are Upāsarā, *i. e.* separate buildings erected by each sect for their monks or nuns. An Upāsaro is a large bare hall without bathrooms or cooking places, furnished only with wooden beds. These beds the monks or nuns are forbidden by their rule to possess, but they are lent for an indefinite period by charitable lay people, who do not expect to get them back again. The beds occasionally have the name of the lenders carved on them, that there may be no doubt as to whom the merit of lending them belongs.

The Upasaro.

The ascetics live on the alms of the charitable, and as each of the three sects have rather different rules for begging, it may be worth going into the subject in detail.

Begging.

No ascetics of any sect may sit in a layman's house to eat food; nor will they accept food specially cooked for them, but only some of that which is being prepared for the household, and they are never allowed to knock at closed doors, but only to enter doors already opened.

Svetāmbara will usually accept food from people of the Vāṇiā, Brāhman and Kṣatriya caste; in Gujarat however they will not accept food from Kṣatriya.

Sthānakavāsi, failing Vāṇiā and Brāhmans, will accept food from the Shepherd caste.

Neither a Svetāmbara nor a Sthānakavāsi will accept food taken to the Upāsaro for them by a layman. The Svetāmbara, however, will accept an invitation to go to a layman's house in order to fetch food and to take it back to the Upāsaro; this a Sthānakavāsi will not do.

In the Bombay Gazetteer* it is stated that the Dhundhiā priests do not beg; this however my Dhundhiā (*i. e.* Sthānakavāsi) friends assure me is unfortunately not the case.

The householders who are begged from feel obliged to give, and the support of so large a body of mendicants is felt as a very severe tax by a great number of thrifty and hard working Hindus and Jaina. A Brāhman gentleman, who though of good position had to strain every nerve to make both ends meet, told me that it cost him at least a rupee a week to satisfy all the religious mendicants who begged from him, a sum equivalent to four days' labour.

* Vol. ix. Part I. p. 106.

JAINA LAY ADHERENTS.

One of the reasons for the total disappearance of Buddhism from India under the stress of Mahommedan invasion and Brahmanic spiritual pressure was its failure to connect itself with its lay adherents by sufficiently close bonds. This mistake Jainism never made: the famous Mathurā inscriptions record the dedication by lay men and lay women of Jaina statues to Jaina temples under the direction of some Jaina monk or nun, and shew clearly that at that early date (probably A. D. 83–176) the S'rāvaka* or lay adherents formed an integral part of the Jaina organisation.†

The Twelve Vows of Laymen

Jaina laymen to day take twelve vows (*Bāra Vrata* બાર વ્રત), the first five of which, as will be seen, resemble the five great vows of monks, modified to suit the different circumstances of lay life.‡

---

* *i. e.* hearers.

† See Dr. Hoernle's Annual Address. A. S. B. 1898. pp. 50, ff.

‡ Jaina are occasionally found in positions (as for example in the police, or in earlier times in the army) where the taking of life becomes part of their official duty. They are not then forbidden to carry out these duties, but while remaining in such positions would not be considered true S'rāvaka. The classic instance given by the Jaina themselves is King Kumārpāla, who, though a convinced Jaina, frequently for many years engaged in battle. This was before he had taken the vows, for after taking them, he never went to battle to the end of his life, though reserving to himself the right, if occasion arose, to fight strictly in self defence, which indeed had been his practice throughout.

1. Ahimsa'. The layman takes in a looser form the vow not to destroy life; thus he is allowed to use certain vegetables (though they are considered to possess one life), and fuel for cooking.

Unhappily this vow does not seem to carry with it any obligation of kindness to animals, beyond refraining from actually taking their lives.

The taking of this vow, has had a most unfortunate effect on the Jaina character. It has cut them off from agriculture (since ploughing, reaping, etc., destroy much insect life), blacksmithing and most of the manufacturing trades. This has thrust them into commerce, and especially into its least elevating branch of money lending. Most of the money lending in Western India is in the hands of the Jaina, and this accounts in a great measure both for their unpopularity and for their wealth.

Of course the Jaina, though they may not engage in agriculture, live on its products,* indeed it seems impossible to escape profiting, even unwillingly, by the universal law of sacrifice.

2. Truth. The laity take the vow against lying, but in a very limited form which allows for the exigencies of commercial or professional life.

3. Honesty. In the same way they take the vow against stealing in such a form as "approves all forms of competition."

---

* In certain parts of Western India a great deal of the best land has passed into the hands of Jaina through their money-lending transactions. This land they rent to farmers and thus very literally live on the products of agriculture.

4. Chastity.

Instead of celibacy, they promise to be faithful to their wife or wives. The Svetāmbara allow remarriage during the wife's life-time if there be no issue by the first wife; the Digambara on the other hand, at least in certain localities, to their honour dissent from this practice, and do not allow a man to marry a second wife while his first is still alive.

5. Against Covetousness.

In his fifth vow the layman promises to set limits to his covetousness with regard to land and houses, money, coin, servants, cattle and plenishing.

6. Dis′ivrata Parima′na.

The sixth vow taken by laymen is that of *Dis′ivrata Parimāṇa* (દિશિવ્રત પરિમાણ). In this vow a man binds himself for life to keep within a certain space. My pandit told me that he, for example, had vowed never during this life time to go beyond England on the one side or Japan on the other, never to go further north than the Himalayas or further south than Ceylon. So far as I could judge, he would never have the least opportunity of breaking his vow, but he told me that if it were for a religious reason he could do so without sin.

7. Upabhoga Paribhoga Parima′na.

The seventh vow, the *Upabhoga Paribhoga Parimāṇa* (ઉપભોગ પરિભોગ પરિમાણ), also lasts for a life time. By it a man fixes what food, clothes or furniture he will use. My pandit, for instance, had vowed that he would never use more than fifty things. The fewer things one can manage to use the better.

The duration of the eighth vow, the *Anartha Daṇḍa*

Vrata (અનર્થ દંડ વ્રત) is generally for life, but sometimes for only five or ten years. One promises for the fixed period not to think evil of any one, not to be too overjoyed at the good fortune of any one, not to be careless in one's work, and not to keep more weapons than are necessary, and to keep those in safe places.

8. Anartha Danda Vrata.

The ninth vow, *Sāmāyika* (સામાયિક), relates to one's religious duties. One promises in it to spend a certain portion of time in meditation every day or every year.

9. Sa'ma'yika.

The tenth vow, *Des'āvakās'ika Vrata* (દેશાવકાશિક વ્રત), is taken for one day only; one vows to limit the space he will travel over, to increase the period of meditation either at home or in the Upāsaro, and to decrease the number of things he will use on that particular day.

10. Des'a'va-ka's'ika Vrata.

The effect of the eleventh vow, *Poṣadha Vrata* (પોષધ વ્રત) must be to connect the laity still closer with the monastic order, for in it one promises to lead a monk's life for a day. This means (in practice) to fast from food and drink for that period.

11. Posadha Vrata.

The twelfth vow, *Atithi Saṁvibhāga Vrata* (અતિથિ સંવિભાગ વ્રત), must be equally useful to the monastic orders, for in it the layman promises to set aside every day a special portion of food for the poor or for ascetics.

12. Alms.

Caste and Customs.

The Jaina say that Mahāvira's second great message

to mankind was that *Kurma* was of far greater importance than caste. If this were ever the case, the message has lost its power now, for the Jaina are perhaps the most caste-ridden people in India.* Some years ago it was commonly believed by European scholars that both Buddhism and Jainism were revolts against the tyranny of caste in general, but unfortunately they seem to have been merely revolts of the higher castes against Brahmanic exclusiveness, which shut the door of the highest *ās'rama* against all but Brāhman ascetics.

Caste.

Dr. Bühler† says that " the characteristic feature of this religion is its claim to universality, which it holds in common with Buddhism and in opposition to Brahmanism. It also declares its object to be to lead all men to salvation, and to open its arms—not only to the noble Aryan, but also to the low-born S'udra and even to the alien, deeply despised in India, the Mlechha." If it ever had such kindly feeling to the low castes, Jainism now most effectually " dissembles its love." At two of the great centres of Jaina pilgrimage, Mt. Abu and Girnār, I was assured that no low caste would be allowed to enter their temples to worship.‡ And today, when all that is most generous and enlightened in young India is longing to free itself from the huge incubus of caste that is thwarting all true development, not one of the Jaina associations dare put on the programme of its Conference any motion in favour of the relaxation of caste restrictions.

---

* Imperial Gazetteer of India. Vol. I. p. 416.

† The Indian sect of the Jainas. p. 3.

‡ A Parsi who some years ago became a Jaina was for long not allowed to enter their temples to worship, and even now no Jaina can eat with him.

This is due not to the laity so much as to the obscurantism of the ascetics, who at their initiation were themselves supposed to have renounced caste. The Mathurā inscriptions bear witness to the antiquity of caste amongst the Jaina,* but to the cruelty and inhumanity of it I know no more convincing testimony than the notice in English affixed to the entrance of Haṭhisiṁha's temple in Ahmedabad, which runs as follows:—

"Low caste servants in attendance on visitors and dogs cannot be allowed to enter the temple."

The Brahmans are still the domestic chaplains of the Jaina, and officiate at their wedding, birth and death ceremonies. The Brahmanic ritual is followed almost completely in the case of a Jaina wedding, excepting that of late years, instead of fire, Arihanta is worshipped, a change due to the influence of the conferences.

Marriage.

The customary age for marriage differs with the sects: the Sthānakavāsi and Svetāmbara generally marry their daughters at about fourteen or fifteen to boys of about nineteen or twenty. There is however no special religious sanction amongst them for any particular age.†

The Digambara are governed by fifty-three rules of life (Saṁskāra સંસ્કાર), and amongst these is a saying that 'a father should seek a fitting husband for his daughter.' They generally marry their daughters when about ten

* Dr. Hoernle's Annual Address. A. S. B. 1898. p. 51.

† Dr. Burgess (Notes on the Jainas. p. 36) says:—"Among Jainas, as among Brahmans, it is strictly prescribed that girls should be betrothed before puberty." The Jaina I have consulted deny this.

or twelve years of age. Vāṇiā sometimes accept money in exchange for their daughters, but this, which practically amounts to selling their own children, is much contemned by other Jaina.*

Svetāmbara, Digambara and Sthānakavāsi will all intermarry if they are of the same caste. They will also intermarry with Hindus of their own caste. Curiously enough, certain Svetāmbara in Ahmedabad will intermarry, but will not dine with, Sthānakavāsi.

Birth.

The birth ceremonies are practically the same as the Brāhman ones. On the sixth day after the child's birth a cloth † is spread, with paper and ink on it, and it is believed that fate then writes on the baby's forehead. On the twelfth day the father's sister names the child, and boiled grain and molasses are distributed. The child's horoscope is deciphered by a Brāhman.

Co-wives.

Amongst the Svetāmbara and Sthānakavāsi, if no child is born, a husband is allowed to remarry, although the first wife be still living. If the second wife bear him no child, he may marry a third and even a fourth. Although this is allowed by custom, it is not really allowed by the Jaina Scriptures,

* The offenders, however, defend themselves by saying that these daughters had in a previous existence been their debtors, and that they had been reborn into their houses as daughters simply to give their creditors this very opportunity of recovering a bad debt!

† The piece of cloth is generally torn from the turban of the oldest man in the family, as it is believed that the child will live as long as he does.

and a man who does so is not considered quite respectable by his fellow castemen.*

The Digambara, as we have already seen, disapprove of remarriage during the life-time of the wife.

Widow Remarriage.

All three sects of Jaina unite in forbidding widow remarriage. They give as a reason that one who has been freed from worldly ties should not seek to form them again; but this reason surely applies just as strongly to the case of men; nevertheless all sects allow widowers to remarry.†

There is, however, one small subsect of the Digambara who permit their widows to remarry and in consequence are much despised by their fellow Jaina. Unfortunately all over India it is considered a sign of good social standing for a caste to disallow widow remarriage.

Purdah.

It is not a Jaina custom to keep women in seclusion, but the practise has been adopted by them as a protection, and also as a sign of good social position, wherever Mahommedan influence is specially strong.

The three sects all permit women to go to their several conferences, and have a Ladies' Day for them.

---

* A Sthānakavāsi Jaina, who thus remarried at Morvi, was recently severely censured by his sect.

† They say that this is because the number of women is twenty seven times as great as that of men; when told that the census absolutely contradicts these figures (since in India for every 1000 males only 963 females are born) they reply: "Oh yes, it isn't true, it's only a reason !!"

Death.

The death ceremonies, which are conducted by a Brāhman, very much resemble those of the Hindus. The Jaina, however, after the dead body has been burnt at the side of a river, pour water over the ashes and simply leave them on the bank, whereas the Brāhmans throw the ashes into the river.

Like the Brāhmans, too, the Jaina bury instead of burning a child of less than a year and a half. The Brāhmans bury their dead ascetics, but the Jaina burn their dead (with the exception of infants) whether lay or ascetics, lest the body should give rise to too much insect life.

The Jaina wear white or black turbans as a sign of mourning, but unlike Gujarāti Brāhmans do not shave their moustaches on the tenth day.

JAINA DOCTRINE.

The Jaina have no belief in one eternal God, supreme Ruler and Creator of the world. They believe the world to be eternal, and give strangely inadequate reasons to prove that it could never have been created. A creator, they say, must have himself had a creator, and so on from eternity; moreover a creator, if there were one, must have created sin and evil, and being thus responsible for the unequal distribution of happiness and unhappiness, have shown a favouritism incompatible with Divinity. They deny the fatherhood of God, and we have seen how the whole system of their caste rules is a negation of the brotherhood of man. Though freely using the titles which other religions reserve for the Supreme Being, they apply them to human beings who have gradually raised themselves to certain peculiarly exalted positions. Beyond this their conceptions do not rise.

Siddha.

They believe that there are five stages through which a human being must generally pass before he can thus become a Siddha. First he must become a *Sādhu* (સાધુ) or ascetic, and then pass on to be an *Upādhyāya* (ઉપાધ્યાય) or Preceptor, when he can teach both laymen and ascetics; next he may become an *A'chārya* (આચાર્ય) and be at the head of a body of monks or ascetics, with powers of ruling and excommunicating. The next highest stage is to become a *Tirthankara* (તીર્થંકર), one who has obtained perfect knowledge and, having crossed the troubled river of constant transmigrations, is at rest. The highest of all is to become a *Siddha* (સિદ્ધ), whom they define as one "without caste, unaffected by smell, without the sense of taste, without feeling, without form, without hunger, without pain, without sorrow, without joy, without birth, without old age, without death, without body, without *Karma*, enjoying endless happiness." That is to say, the "holiest, highest manhood" that the Jaina set before themselves as their ideal is that in which personality is completely stultified.

All life is divided into two classes, *Bhavi* (ભવી) and *Abhavi* (અભવી), according as it has or has not the capacity to become a Siddha, and only a Tirthaṅkara or Kevali knows to which division it belongs.

Tirthankara.

The Tirthaṅkara rather than the Siddha seem to have seized on the popular imagination; it is their images which are in the Jaina temples, and legends of their gigantic stature and lives of interminable length are eagerly repeated.

Certain picturesque miracles are said to have taken place whenever any of the Tirthaṅkara preached on earth; an aśoka tree springs up at the place and grows to twelve times the preacher's height, the dwellers in Devaloka listen to his sermon and scatter flowers from heaven: some gods sing and play celestial music, others wave a fly whisk in front of the preacher. A lion shaped throne and a state umbrella are provided for him by the gods, a halo of light encircles his head, and whenever he pauses to take breath in his discourse, a celestial kettle drum is enthusiastically beaten. A Tirthaṅkara's preaching has thirty-five characteristics, amongst the most important of which, from a hearer's point of view, are that it is always sweet, intelligible, accurate and interesting.

Every Tirthaṅkara has also thirty four bodily characteristics, his blood for instance is white, his body has a sweet odour and he is never seen to eat.

List of Tirthankara.

The following list of Tirthaṅkara of the present age shows some slight differences between the sects.

(1) ṚISABHADEVA (ઋષભદેવ) or A'DINA'THA (આદિનાથ), whose sign is the bull.

(2) AJITANA'THA (અજિતનાથ), whose sign is the elephant.

(3) SAMBHAVANA'THA (સંભવનાથ), whose sign is the horse.

(4) ABHINANDANA (અભિનંદન), whose sign is the ape.

(5) SUMATINA'THA (સુમતિનાથ), whose sign is the red goose.

(6) PADMAPRABHU (પદ્મપ્રભુ), whose sign is the lotus flower.

(7) SUPA'RS'VANA'THA (સુપાર્શ્વનાથ), whose sign is the *svastika* symbol. 卐

(8) CANDRAPRABHU (ચંદ્રપ્રભુ), whose sign is the moon.

(9) SUVIDHINA'THA (સુવિધિનાથ), whose sign is the crocodile [? Digambara : crab].

(10) S'ITALANA'THA (શીતળનાથ), whose sign is the *S'rivatsa* figure [? Digambara : *ficus religiosa*].

(11) S'REYA'ṀSANA'THA (શ્રેયાંસનાથ), whose sign is the rhinoceros.

(12) VA'SUPUJYA (વાસુપૂજ્ય), whose sign is the male buffalo.*

(13) VIMALANA'THA (વિમલનાથ), whose sign is the boar.

* Dr. Burgess in his edition of Dr. Bühler's "Indian sect of the Jainas," p. 69, gives the sign as the female buffalo, but all the Jaina I have asked give the male.

(14) ANANTANA'THA (અનંતનાથ), whose sign is a hawk [? Digambara : a bear].

(15) DHARMANA'THA (ધર્મનાથ), whose sign is a thunderbolt.

(16) S'A'NTINA'THA (શાન્તિનાથ), whose sign is a deer.*

(17) KUNTHUNA'THA (કુંથુનાથ), whose sign is a goat.

(18) ARANA'THA (અરનાથ), whose sign is a step-well [?] †

(19) MALLINA'THA (મલ્લિનાથ), whose sign is a water jar. This the Svetāmbara believe to have been the only woman Tirthaṅkara.‡ The Digambara of course do not hold this, as they do not think a woman can attain Mokṣa.

(20) MUNISUVRATA (મુનિસુવ્રત), whose sign is the tortoise.

(21) NAMINA'THA (નમિનાથ), whose sign is the blue lotus [Digambara : As'oka tree].

(22) NEMINA'THA (નેમિનાથ), whose sign is the conch shell, and to whom Mt. Girnār (in Kāṭhiāwād) is specially sacred.

(29) PA'RS'VANAT'HA (પાર્શ્વનાથ), whose sign is the serpent.

(24) MAHA'VIRA (મહાવીર), whose sign is the lion, the most famous of all the Tirthaṅkara, and whose life we have already given.

Besides Mahāvira, the favourite Tirthaṅkara are Pārs'-vanātha, Neminātha, S'āntinātha and the first, Ṛiṣabhadeva.

---

* Dr. Burgess *loc. cit.* gives antelope.

† Dr. Burgess gives the *Nandyāvarta* diagram.

‡ Some twenty-five years ago her image was found in Bhoyaṇi in Gujarat ; and this has given the place such sanctity that, though quite a small village, it has been chosen as the place of meeting of the S'vetāmbara Conference of 1910.

The names are also recorded of Twenty-four Tirthaṅkara who preceded those of the present age, and of Twenty-four who will succeed them; other sets of Twenty-four Tirthaṅkara will follow these, and so on in endless succession.

Jaina Eschatology.

The Jaina have preserved the Hindu doctrine of Transmigration, though they subdivide the Eighty-four Lakhs (*i. e.* Eighty-four hundred thousand) of rebirths, through which a soul may pass, by an elaborate classification of their own. This doctrine, together with that of Karma, which they also hold in common with the Hindus, colours all their eschatology.

Svarga.

The Jaina heaven, *Svargu* (સ્વર્ગ), is attained by those who have acquired great merit, but who are still subject in some measure to Karma.

In Svarga both happiness and pain are experienced, but happiness preponderates.

Svarga is divided into twenty-six heavens, which are grouped as follows :—

Devaloka (દેવલોક), or the twelve lower heavens, where the gods and goddesses, (Deva, Devi * દેવ, દેવી,) who resemble those of the Hindus, dwell. At the head of these Deva and Devi are the god Indra and the goddess Indrāṇi.

Next above these heavens come the nine heavens called *Greveyikı* (ગ્રેવેયિક); but before a Deva can pass from Devaloka to Greveyika, he must descend to our world and become a man. The gods in these nine heavens are all equal and without a ruler.

---

* Devi only attain to the lower of these twelve heavens.

Above Greveyika is *Anuttara Vimāna* (અનુત્તર વિમાન) a group of five heavens which are inhabited by higher gods, who will attain Mokṣa after the expiry of one age. To pass to Mokṣa, an inhabitant of Anuttara Vimāna would have to descend to our world and become a man and an ascetic.

Moksa.

Above Svarga is the highest region of all, called *Mokṣa* (મોક્ષ); it is attained by those who are completely freed from Karma, and these are generally ascetics.

The denizens of Mokṣa are Siddha (demi-gods) who experience neither pain nor happiness.

We shall have to discuss Mokṣa later, as it ranks as one of the nine elements of Jaina philosophy.

Tiryakaloka.

Our world, or *Tiryakaloka* (તિર્યંકલોક), is situated beneath the lowest Svarga and separates it from Hell. It is made up of two and a half islands, each of which is divided into seven parts (the half island being divided into seven smaller parts), and these twenty-one parts are again subdivided.

On each Island is a district of great importance called *Mahāvideha* (મહાવિદેહ), but no one knows where this district is. During the fifth and sixth ages only those born in this district can attain Mokṣa, and these, too, must first have been ascetics.

Naraka.

Below our world is *Adholoka* (અધોલોક), which contains the Seven Hells or *Naraka* (નરક). Most vivid pictures are published as to the various torments suffered by the denizens of Hell.*

---

* See નારકીનાં ચિત્રો—or Pictures of Hell. (Publishers and Printers not given !)

The first hell, *Ratna Prabhā* (રત્ન પ્રભા), is paved with sharp stones; the second, *S'arkara Prabhā* (શાર્કર પ્રભા), is paved with stones in the shape of sugar loaves; the third, *Vālu Prabhā* (વાલુ પ્રભા), is paved with sand; the fourth, *Panka Prabhā* (પંક પ્રભા), is paved with mud; then follows *Dhumra Prabhā* (ધુમ્ર પ્રભા), which is filled with smoke; the sixth, *Tama Prabhā* (તમ પ્રભા), is absolutely dark; and in the seventh, *Tamatama Prabhā* (તમતમ પ્રભા), the blackness is even more intense.

The inhabitants of all these hells are tormented by wicked Deva and suffer hideous physical torments, being split open, pierced, cut into pieces, or burned; water is offered to them, and when they try and assuage their thirst by drinking it, it turns into molten lead.

They suffer for a fixed period according to their Karma, and are then reborn as men or lower animals or, lowest of all, as some vegetable, perhaps a potato or even an onion!

The Jaina illustrate these divisions by the diagram of a man. His legs are Adholoka with the seven hells, our world, Tiryakaloka, is his waist, and above comes Urdhvaloka (ઉર્ધ્વલોક) or Svarga, his breast being Devaloka, his neck Greveyika and his face Anuttara Vimāna. His crown is Mokṣa.

KARMA.

Jaina, in common with Hindus, believe that *Karma* (action), the accumulated force of a man's actions, good and bad, in previous existences,* not only determines every detail of his present life and future existence,† but necessitates his passing through an unknown succession of rebirths, until his Karma be exhausted.

It is interesting to note that of all the Tirthankara Mahāvira had the greatest accumulation of Karma to exhaust.

The Six Les'a'.

The Jaina believe that there are six emotions or Les'ā which lead to Karma; three are bad, and three are good.

(1) *Kṛiṣṇa Les'ā* (કૃષ્ણ લેશા), or the feeling that gives rise to very evil thoughts; this is the worst of the three bad emotions.

(2) *Nila Les'ā* (નીલ લેશા), the emotion that leads to evil thoughts, but thoughts less evil than the first.

---

* Compare :—

" The Karma—all that total of a Soul
Which is the things it did, the thoughts it had,
The 'self' it wove—with woof of viewless time,
Crossed on the warp of invisible acts—
The outcome of him on the Universe." Sir Edwin Arnold.

† The Hindus constantly quote the saying from the Mahābhārata that " As a calf immediately finds out its mother among many thousands, so does the fruit of actions done in bygone ages follow the agent."

(3) *Kāpota Les'ā* (કાપોત લેશા): this feeling leads to thoughts, evil indeed, but less black than in the first and second case.

The Jaina, it will be noticed, appear to consider the stronghold of evil to lie in the thoughts as much as in the will.

There are three good emotions :—

(1) *Tejo Les'ā* (તેજો લેશા), the remover of evil thoughts, as darkness is banished by light.

(2) *Padma Les'ā* (પદ્મ લેશા). As a lotus flower expands with the rays of the sun, so Tejo Les'ā, coming into the mind, expands it, and this, the next higher emotion, is born.

(3) *S'ukla Les'ā* (શુક્લ લેશા). Under the influence of this emotion the mind itself becomes a sun, and there is no dark corner left which could contain evil thoughts.

The Jaina illustrate the six Les'ā by a parable (more illuminating to the Eastern than the Western mind) of six men who wish to eat mangoes.* The first man under the influence of Kṛṣṇa Les'ā wishes to cut down the whole tree to eat one mango; the man swayed by Nila Les'ā thinks of cutting off a big branch; Kāpota Les'ā induces the third to think of cutting off a smaller branch.

The better influence of Tejo Les'ā suggests to its possessor to pluck off the unripe fruit; Padma Les'ā induces the fifth to propose plucking off those ready to fall; but

---

* This is such a favourite parable that pictures of it are frequently found in Jaina books; the point of it being that, according to Jaina belief, the life, which pervades the branches and unripe fruit, is in the ripe fruit concentrated in the stone, to which no injury is done by eating the fruit.

S'ukla Les'ā persuades the sixth man to think only of picking up those fruits that have fallen down.

The Eight Karma.

The Jaina seem to have a passion for classifying, dividing and subdividing all the tenets of their faith. Karma, which is one of their main doctrines, they classify under eight heads.

1. Jna'na'varaniya Karma.

Jñānāvaraṇiya Karma (જ્ઞાનાવરણીય કર્મ), or the curtain that hides knowledge. If a man is prevented from getting knowledge in one life, either by poverty or stupidity, the reason is that in a previous birth he must have hindered another from getting knowledge; *e. g.* destroyed useful books, or neglected to help a poor student by paying his fees, and so accumulated the Karma which now prevents him from getting knowledge himself.

2. Dars'ana'-varaniya Karma.

Dars'anāvaraṇiya Karma (દર્શનાવરણીય કર્મ). If one man is beginning to believe in the Jaina religion and another hinders him and puts stumbling blocks in his way, the hinderer in his next birth will not be able to have faith even if he longs to possess it. The accumulation of this Karma accounts for the action of those Jaina who eat meat and break the rules of their religion.

3. Vedaniya Karma.

Vedaniya Karma (વેદનીય કર્મ) is the one that brings happiness or unhappiness in the next birth.

Mohaniya Karma (મોહનીય કર્મ), the fourth, is the strongest of all and the one which brings most punishment.

4. Mohaniya Karma. It is accumulated through entanglement in worldly attachments. If a man in one birth is so absorbed in worldly ties that he never thinks of religion, he will be kept away in the next birth from those he loves.

A'yu Karma (આયુ કર્મ) fixes the period during which a man will experience heaven or hell or earthly life. In

5. A'yu Karma. each birth man is building up his A'yu Karma for his next life. A'yu Karma cannot be accumulated beyond one rebirth.

Nāma Karma (નામ કર્મ) decides whether a man will

6. Na'ma Karma. be reborn as an animal or a bird, whether in hell or as a god, *i. e.* in which *Gati** he will be reborn.

Gotra Karma (ગોત્ર કર્મ). A man's actions in one life decide in what caste he will be born in the next: thus by

7. Gotra Karma. doing good to others, by looking always at the bright side of people, or by taking an interest in animal asylums he can try to avoid being born in a low caste, and even hope to be born in one of the highest castes.

Antarāya Karma (અન્તરાય કર્મ). If in one life a man has money and is not willing to spend it on others, or if he

8. Antara'ya Karma. has influence or energy and yet refuses to serve others, he will in his next birth be born without money, influence or energy.

---

* There are four *Gati* : Manuṣya Gati (મનુષ્ય ગતિ), Deva Gati (દેવ ગતિ), Tiryañca Gati (તીર્યંચ ગતિ), and Nāraki Gati (નારકી ગતિ), and they are frequently represented by the *Svastika* symbol.

These eight are subdivided again into one hundred and fifty-eight divisions, into which it is scarcely necessary to go.

The Fourteen Steps to Liberation.

The Jaina believe that a soul is liberated from Karma by fourteen steps, and these they call the *Cauda Guṇasthānaka* (ચૌદ ગુણસ્થાનક.)

The First Step is the *Mithyātva Guṇasthānaka* (મિથ્યાત્વ ગુણસ્થાનક). Men or women, according to the Jaina, often begin to take their first interest in religion by realising that what is unreal is real. Those who are at this stage are completely under bondage to Karma.

1st Step.

Sāsvādana Guṇasthānaka (સાસ્વાદન ગુણસ્થાનક). A man begins to realize what the truths of Jainism are, but finds them too difficult to believe and is still tied down by Karma.

2nd Step.

Mis′ra Guṇasthānaka (મિશ્ર ગુણસ્થાનક). At this stage a man, though continuing to be bound by Karma, begins to hold some truth along with the untruth he still believes.

3rd Step.

Avirati Samyakadṛiṣṭi Guṇasthānaka (અવિરતિ સમ્યકદૃષ્ટિ ગુણસ્થાનક). A man who has reached this stage begins to understand the evils of *excessive* Anger, Pride, Deceit and Greed, and is freed from the three ties of Self righteousness, Self esteem and Self conceit; if these evil qualities are not absolutely destroyed at this stage, they become quiescent and are no longer motives in deciding his conduct. He is now somewhat freed from the chains of Karma.

4th Step.

Des'avirati (*Saṁyatāsaṁyata*) *Guṇasthānaka* (દેશવિરતિ સંયતાસંયત ગુણસ્થાનક). At this point *moderate* Anger, Pride, Deceit and Greed are destroyed or become quiescent in a man, who is now a little more freed from Karma and can take the vows upon himself, either one or all twelve.

5th Step.

Pramatta Guṇasthanaka (પ્રમત્ત ગુણસ્થાનક). *Slight* Anger, Pride, Deceit and Greed are now destroyed or quiescent, and a man will spontaneously desire to keep the vows.

6th Step.

Apramatta Guṇasthānaka (અપ્રમત્ત ગુણસ્થાનક). Anger is now completely destroyed in a man or else remains quiescent. Pride, Deceit and Greed only remain with him in the fourth degree, and he is also, happily, freed from all the bad qualities that would make him lazy or sleepy.

7th Step.

Niyatibādara Guṇasthānaka [*Apurvakaraṇa*] (નિયતિબાદર ગુણસ્થાનક [અપૂર્વકરણ]). This is a particularly interesting stage, as the Digambara believe it to be the highest a woman can reach. The Svetāmbara and Sthānakavāsi, however, believe that a woman can pass through all the stages and attain Mokṣa.

8th Step.

One who has reached this point is freed from Pride, or it remains quiescent. His mind and body are now so disciplined that he can dispense with the aid that the taking of vows affords to his weaker brethren. This stage is called the "Unique" because so few attain to it.

Aniyatibādara Guṇasthānaka (અનિયતિબાદર ગુણસ્થાનક). At this stage a man becomes practically sexless, and he is freed from the dominion of Deceit.

9th Step.

10th Step.

Sukṣmasamparāya Guṇasthānaka (સૂક્ષ્મસંપરાય ગુણ-સ્થાનક). All sense of humour now vanishes from a man, together with his power of feeling grief and—quaint juxtaposition !—his sense of smell.

11th Step.

Upas'ānta Moha Guṇasthānaka (ઉપશાન્ત મોહ ગુણસ્થાનક). It is at this point that Greed should, if not destroyed, at least become quiescent. This is considered a very critical stage : if Greed really dies out, all is well ; but if it be only dormant, and something rouses it, it may drag a man down again. Curiously enough, if he falls, it is not to any of the three stages immediately below him, but to the sixth or seventh stage, or he may even fall as low as the first.

Should a man die in this stage without Greed having been reawakened, he will become an Anuttaravāsi Deva (અનુત્તરવાસી દેવ), *i. e.*, one who after one more rebirth will become a Siddha.

12th Step.

Kṣiṇamoha Guṇasthānaka. (ક્ષીણમોહ ગુણસ્થાનક). At this point a man is freed from four of the Eight Karma (*i. e.* Jñānāvaraṇiya, Dars'anāvaraṇiya Mohaniya and Antarāya), and though the other four remain, they have no more power over him " than a burnt up string." No one can ever die in this stage, for even *in articulo mortis* he would pass through the next two stages and enter Mokṣa.

13th Step.

Sayogi Kevali Guṇasthānaka (સયોગી કેવલી ગુણસ્થાનક). A man who reaches this stage becomes a Kevali, is omniscient, and will at death become a Siddha. (Only the Kevali know which stage a man has reached, but as they take no interest, no one prays to them for aid in getting free from Karma).

A monk who faithfully performs his vows, etc., can reach this thirteenth stage. A layman could reach it, but it would be very hard for him. The S'vetāmbara and Sthānakavāsi, as we have seen, say that it might be reached by a woman, but it would be hardest of all for her. They say that for every 108 men who attain Mokṣa, at most only twenty women do so, and ten neuters.

Ayogi Kevali Guṇasthānaka (અયેાગી કેવલી ગુણસ્થાનક).

14th Step.

No one who has attained the fourteenth and final stage ever lives in it, but, being freed from all Karma, dies at once and becomes a Siddha.

THE NINE CATEGORIES OF JAINA DOCTRINES.

The S'vetāmbara and Sthānakavāsi believe that there are nine principles of Jainism, *Nava Tatva* (નવ તત્વ); the Digambara hold that there are only seven.

i. Jiva (જીવ).

With the Jaina the word Jiva seems to mean sometimes soul, sometimes living being, sometimes consciousness and sometimes vitality.* There are, they say, ten different kinds of life.

Ekendriya.

(1) *Ekendriya* (એકેંદ્રિય). Under this heading are classed things possessed of existence alone. This class is again subdivided into things *visible* (bādara બાદર), as a stone, clay, wind, water, fire, and certain vegetables as onions; and things *invisible* (sukṣma સૂક્ષ્મ), as, for example, oxygen. It is the fear of injuring these Ekendriya that so limits the trades a Jaina can follow. Children are even forbidden to play with any of these, such as stones or lumps of earth, for fear of injuring them.†

Be Indriya.

(2) *Be Indriya* (બે ઇંદ્રિય). Living things possessed, the Jaina say, of body and tongue have two senses, as caterpillars, leeches, worms, animalculae.

---

* જૈન ધર્મ પ્રવેશ પોથી. Part 2. p. 38. This is one of a Gujarati Series of books of instruction in the Jaina religion prepared for children, and published at Ahmedabad in 1907.

† Id. Part 1. p. 28.

(3) *Tri Indriya* (ત્રિ ઇંદ્રિય). Things in this class possess one extra 'sense' besides body and tongue, *i. e.* nose.

Tri Indriya.

In each class the extra 'sense' which distinguishes it from the class below is supposed to be the one which exercises the most power. In this division the Jaina put ants, bugs, moths, black ants. An unfortunate result of this is that the Jaina will not kill vermin.

(4) *Corendriya* (ચોરેંદ્રિય). The things which possess

Corendriya.

body, tongue, nose and eyes are considered to be four sensed; they include scorpions, butterflies, locusts, wasps, bees, mosquitoes.

(5) *Pañcendriya* (પંચેંદ્રિય). In the fifth class things possess body, tongue, nose, eyes and ears. They are divided

Pancendriya.

into two classes, those possessing 'intelligence,' Sañjñi Pañcendriya (સંજ્ઞી પંચેંદ્રિય), as men, gods, certain birds and beasts; and those without intelligence, Asañjñi Pañcendriya (અસંજ્ઞી પંચેંદ્રિય), certain other birds and beasts, frogs, fishes, germs (of plague) etc.

All five classes are subdivided into two divisions, in which things are placed according as time is necessary for

Double Division.

the full development of the 'senses' or as the senses are fully developed at birth. Thus if a child dies before birth, though it belongs to the highest division, it is classed as undeveloped (Aparyāptā અપર્યાપ્તા). For a man to be developed (Paryāptā પર્યાપ્તા) he must possess six things :—Food (A'hāra આહાર), Body (S'arira શરીર), Senses (Indriya ઇંદ્રિય), Speech (Bhāṣā ભાષા), Mind (Mana મન) and Respiration (S'vāsocchvāsa શ્વાસો-ચ્છ્વાસ).

ii. Ajiva (અજીવ).

The Jaina make five divisions in the class of things "without life," and these with Jiva make up the whole of the universe.*

1. Motion. *Dharmāstikāya* (ધર્માસ્તિકાય): Motion, for example that which, brought into connection with a fish, makes it swim.

2. Inertia. *Adharmāstikāya* (અધર્માસ્તિકાય): Inertia in soul or body.

3. Space. *A'kāś'āstikāya* (આકાશાસ્તિકાય): Space.

4. Time. *Kāḷa* (કાળ): Time.

The Jaina make two divisions in time:—

(*a*) *Vyavahārika Kāḷa* (વ્યવહારીક કાળ), which includes the ordinary divisions of time into days, years etc., and (*b*) *Addhāsamaya Kāḷa* (અદ્ધાસમય કાળ), or time which works alterations, *e. g.* which makes new things old and old new.

5. Form. *Pudgaḷāstikāya* (પુદ્ગળાસ્તિકાય). Under this heading is included every thing that relates to our means of perception, such as colour, touch, smell and taste. The Jaina believe that there are five primary colours, *viz*:—red, yellow, blue (or green), black and white. Under "touch," (સ્પર્શ) they classify things heavy and light, smooth and rough, dry and wet, hot and cold.

---

* The late Rev. Douglas Thoronton has well said:—"These are vaguely classed and generally incapable of interpretation." Parsi, Jāina and Sikh, p. 63.

iii. The Forty two A's'rava.

There are forty-two A's'rava (આશ્રવ) or Paths leading to the Eight Karma, and of these seventeen are major and twenty-five minor. The current Jaina illustration of A's'rava is as follows:—the soul is like a tank into which, like water through rills and channels, Karma flows by way of the body, tongue, nose, eyes and ears.* Of the seventeen major A's'rava, four are included under:—

The Passions.

Kaṣāya (કષાય) or passions, namely Anger, (Krodha ક્રોધ), Pride (Māna માન), Illusion (Māyā માયા), Greed (Lobha લોભ). These are all subdivided according to their extent. In the case of Anger (which they believe dwells in the forehead) there are:—

(1) *Anantānubandhi* (અનંતાનુબન્ધી), or the bitterest anger, which is endless, and the punishment for which is Hell.

(2) *Apacakhāṇāvaraṇiya* (અપચ્ચખાણાવરણીય), or anger which lasts for not more than a year, and which is ended on the Jaina festival of good will, the last day of Pajjusaṇa. If a man die whilst he is indulging in this anger, he will become a beast or bird.

(3) *Pacakhāṇāvaraṇiya* (પચ્ચખાણાવરણીય), or anger which lasts for not more than fifteen days.

At the end of every fifteen days there is a special confession of sin amongst the Jaina, and this anger must end then. If a man die in this state, he will have no chance of becoming a saint in his next birth, but will be born a man.

---

* જૈન ધર્મ પ્રવેશ પોથી. Part 2. p. 59.

(4) *Sañjvalana* (સંજ્વલન), or slight anger. This anger is confessed and dismissed at the end of every day at the evening confession. If a man die whilst indulging in this form of anger, he cannot become a Siddha, but might be a Tirthankara in his next birth.

Pride, Illusion and Greed are divided in the same way and carry the same punishments.

The *Pāñca Indriya* (પાંચ ઇંદ્રિય). The next five A'srava consist in failing to restrain the senses of sight, hearing, smell, taste and touch. Though the immediate results of exercising these senses may be good, yet they lead to entanglement.

The Senses.

The *Pāñca Avrata* (પાંચ અવ્રત) are the opposites of the five great vows, and consist of killing, lying, stealing, unchastity and coveting.

Breach of Vows.

The remaining three, the *Traṇa Yoga* (ત્રણ યોગ), come from failing to restrain body, mind and speech.

Trana Yoga.

The Digambara include under A'srava *Merit* (Puṇya પુણ્ય) and *Sin* (Pāpa પાપ), which, unlike the Svetāmbara and Sthānakavāsi, they do not consider to be main divisions of the nine categories, but only subdivisions.

iv. Samvara (સંવર): the Impeding of Karma.

The Jaina believe that Karma may be impeded in fifty-seven ways. Ten of these we have already learnt under the Ten duties of monks and nuns ; besides these there are:—

Five Rules of Conduct (*Pāñca Samiti* પાંચ સમિતિ) which impede Karma :—

(1) *Iryā Samiti* (ઇર્યા સમિતિ), *i. e.* walking carefully and avoiding treading on anything.

Rules of Conduct.

(2) *Bhāṣā Samiti* (ભાષા સમિતિ), or speaking sweet, wholesome, true words.

(3) *Esaṇā Samiti* (એષણા સમિતિ): taking only such food as is allowed by the S'āstras and avoiding the forty-two sins of eating.

(4) *A'dānanikṣepaṇā Samiti* (આદાનનિક્ષેપણા સમિતિ): sweeping the ground to clear it of insects before sitting down.

(5) *Parithāpanikā Samiti* (પરિથાપનિકા સમિતિ): right disposal of refuse.

Three Gupti.

The Three *Gupti* (ગુપ્તિ) also impede Karma; they are strictly binding on monks and nuns, and also, though more loosely, on the laity. They are:—

(1) *Manogupti* (મનોગુપ્તિ), or controlling the mind: a monk must give up wandering thoughts and fix the mind on meditation.

(2) *Vacanagupti* (વચનગુપ્તિ), controlling the speech: a monk should speak as little as possible and occasionally vow silence for a whole day.

(3) *Kāyagupti* (કાયગુપ્તિ), restraining bodily movement. If a monk is meditating, he should not start even if a snake appear; whenever he moves, he should take care not to injure any living thing.

The Twenty-two Parisaha.

There are also Twenty-two Ways of Endurance or *Parisaha* (પરિસહ), by which a monk or nun is bound, and the laity should endeavour, to impede Karma. (Such endurance is specially binding on the laity during the Poṣadha Vow). The monk must endure hunger (*Kṣudhā Pariṣaha* ક્ષુધા પરિસહ); thirst (*Tṛiṣā* તૃષા), only drinking hot fluids; cold (*S'ita* શીત), without lighting a fire or asking for extra clothing; heat (*Uṣṇa* ઉષ્ણ), without even fanning; mosquito bites (*Dāṁsa* ડાંસ); unsuitable clothing (*Vastra* વસ્ત્ર); he must be indifferent to the lodging, food, clothes, etc., he obtains (*Arati,* અરતિ); indifferent to women (*Stri* સ્ત્રી); he must not mind changing his dwelling (*Caryā* ચર્યા); must be indifferent to danger and fear (*Nais'idhiki* નૈશિધિકી); as to getting a bed or not (*S'ayyā* શય્યા); must endure taunts, etc. (*A'kros'a* આક્રોશ); beating (*Vadha* વધ); unkindness when begging (*Yāñcā* યાંચા); refusal when begging (*Alābha* અલાભ); illness (*Roga* રોગ); must not mind the prickly grass on which he lies (*Triṇasparśa* તૃણસ્પર્શ); must endure dirt on his body (*Mela* મેલ); must not be puffed up when praised for his learning or virtue (*Satkāra* સત્કાર); nor proud whilst teaching his pupils (*Prajñā* પ્રજ્ઞા); must not remember his learning and his studies (*Ajñāna* અજ્ઞાન); and finally, must never allow a doubt as to the truth of his religion any foot-hold in his mind (*Samyaktva Pariṣaha* સમ્યક્ત્વ પરિસહ).

Twelve great reflections (*Bhāvanā* ભાવના) must be remembered, especially by monks and nuns, but also by the laity :—

Twelve Reflections.

(1) *Anitya Bhāvanā* (અનિત્ય ભાવના): One must constantly remember that the world is transitory and the soul eternal.

(2) *As'araṇa Bhāvanā* (અશરણ ભાવના): that the soul fears death and has no shelter.

(3) *Saṁsāra Bhāvanā* (સંસાર ભાવના): that man is constantly taking birth.

(4) *Ekatva Bhāvanā* (એકત્વ ભાવના): that the soul came unaccompanied, goes unaccompanied and must suffer for its actions.

(5) *Anyatva Bhāvanā* (અન્યત્વ ભાવના): that neither wealth, son nor wife are really ours but belong to others.

(6) *As'auca Bhāvanā* (અશૌચ ભાવના): that even our body is not our own and is impure.

(7) *A's'rava Bhāvanā* (આશ્રવ ભાવના). One must reflect how hard it is to be free from Karma when sin may lurk in one's every action.

(8) *Saṁvara Bhāvanā* (સંવર ભાવના): that to destroy Karma one must take certain vows, either small or great.

(9) *Nirjarā Bhāvanā* (નિર્જરા ભાવના). In order to completely destroy Karma one must meditate on austerities.

(10) *Loka Bhāvanā* (લોક ભાવના). One must think of the world as in the form of a man. Instead of searching for God in anything one must think of himself as capable of becoming a Siddha.

(11) *Bodhibija Bhāvanā* (બોધિબીજ ભાવના). One must think how he shall take the first step in his religion, and then go on mounting.

(12) *Dharma Bhāvanā* (ધર્મ ભાવના): and he must think of the highest truth in his religion, and be thankful that he was born a Jaina.

Finally, there are five Rules of Conduct or Discipline, *Cāritra* (ચારિત્ર), which impede Karma :—

Five Ca'ritra.

(1) *Sāmāyika Cāritra* (સામાયિક ચારિત્ર), the giving up of all sinful actions and performing innocent ones, and looking on all mankind as equal.

(2) *Chedopasthāpaniya Cāritra* (છેદોપસ્થાપનીય ચારિત્ર), repenting for all sins.

(3) *Parihāra Vis'uddha Cāritra* (પરિહાર વિશુદ્ધ ચારિત્ર). This third rule is variously given by the various sects; it may mean to go when ordered by a superior to a miserable place as a test of endurance.

(4) *Sukṣmasamparāya Cāritra* (સૂક્ષ્મસંપરાય ચારિત્ર). To try and have very little attachment to this world. There are, as we saw, fourteen stages on the way to Liberation, and he who is thus but lightly tied to this world has reached the tenth stage.

(5) *Yathākhyāta Cāritra* (યથાખ્યાત ચારિત્ર). The fifth rule of conduct is carried out when one has lost *all* attachment to the world and thinks only of the soul. This is to attain the thirteenth and fourteenth stages towards Liberation.

v. Nirjara' (નિર્જરા.)

The fifth great principle or category of Jainism deals with the partial destruction of Karma. It is effected by those exterior and interior austerities which we have already discussed under *Tapa* when we were studying the ten duties of monks and nuns.*

vi. Bandha (બંધ.)

The sixth principle is also concerned with Karma and our bondage to it. Each of the eight Karma already mentioned† is considered with regard to its nature, duration, quality and quantity.

---

* See page 34. † See page 59.

Karma is also classified with regard to time into *Sattā* (સત્તા), that which accumulated in a past life; *Bandha* (બંધ), that accumulated in the present life, and *Udaya* (ઉદય), that of which the effects are now being experienced. (The Vedantists, though they call them by different names, have these three last classifications).

If Jaina believed in Karma alone, it would lead to such absolute fatalism that all present activity would be stultified. " What " people would ask " is the use of bestirring oneself when all one's life has been decided by the actions of some previous existence." To counteract this tendency they teach that Karma is divided into two parts.

(1) *Nikācita* (નિકાચિત), or the Karma whose results we are in any case obliged to experience.

(2) *S'ithila* (શિથિલ), or the Karma from whose effects we may escape by extraordinary exertions. As no one knows to which class his Karma belongs, he is incited to activity in the hope of avoiding calamities.

vii. Moksa.

The seventh Jaina principle deals with Mokṣa (મોક્ષ)* or complete deliverance. When Mokṣa is attained, one is absolutely freed from the effects of the eight Karma and from rebirth. Very few women ever attain it, as they are not gifted with sufficient powers of body or mind, but a non-Jaina who had kept even accidentally all the tenets of Jainism might reach it.

These seven principles are held in common by all Jaina; the Digambara, however, as we have seen before, do not hold the two following to be main principles.

* See also page 54.

viii. Punya.

Puṇya (પુણ્ય) or merit can be earned in any of the following nine ways :—

Nine ways of Earning Merit. (1) *Anna Puṇya* (અન્ન પુણ્ય): giving food to the poor or to mendicants.

(2) *Pāṇa Puṇya* (પાણી પુણ્ય): giving water to the thirsty. *Cold* water can never be given to ascetics, and the hot water given must be surplus hot water, and not water specially warmed for them.

(3) *Layaṇa Puṇya* (લયણ પુણ્ય): building houses for the homeless, or setting aside special buildings for ascetics. Jaina monks from Mālwā and Mārwār will never stay at an Upāsaro (monastery), but beg the loan of empty houses. They are afraid, if they used one specially erected for them, of sharing in the guilt of building houses (by which life may have been destroyed).

(4) *S'ayaṇa Puṇya* (શયણ પુણ્ય): providing seats, beds or bedding for those who are in need. It is in order to earn this merit that laymen lend to an Upāsaro the broad benches the monks sleep on.

(5) *Vastra Puṇya* (વસ્ત્ર પુણ્ય): merit gained by giving clothing to the poor and naked, or renewing the five garments permitted to a monk.

(6) *Mana Puṇya* (મન પુણ્ય): thinking well of others. It is considered very meritorious to think of the "bright side" of other people, and to remember their good qualities whilst forgetting their bad. One should also constantly plan to promote the happiness of others.

(7) *Vacana Puṇya* (વચન પુણ્ય): speaking well of and to others. This includes merit gained by speaking as highly as possible of others, giving them good advice, instruction, lectures etc, and always speaking politely.

(8) *S'arira Puṇya* (શરીર પુણ્ય): serving others at some bodily trouble to oneself, and personally looking after the sick and aged. A layman cannot thus serve monks, who must be served by their brother monks; if, however, a layman has taken the Poṣadha vow,* he can serve a monk as long as the vow lasts.

(9) *Namaskāra Puṇya* (નમસ્કાર પુણ્ય): showing reverence to elders, superiors and ascetics. One can acquire this form of merit by bowing, by salaaming with both hands, and by generally showing reverence in bodily postures.

The fruit of Punya.

The fruit of Puṇya is divided into fifty-two classes of rewards, which vary according to the zeal with which the action was performed. Some actions, for instance, bring fame, some health of body or beauty of form or voice, others assure your being born in an exalted family, or even win Mokṣa, and the highest of all raises the doer to the rank of a Tirthaṅkara.

Although the Jaina have set before themselves so complete a system of altruism, and buttressed it by rewards appealing so strongly to self interest, it seems to have but little influence on their conduct to any but Jaina and ascetics. The callous indifference to human suffering shown by this rich community during the famine which devastated

---

* See page 43.

Gujarat in 1900* has left an indelible stain on a reputation already tarnished by their apathy regarding infanticide.

The practice of female infanticide was, before the British Government intervened to put an end to it, almost universal amongst certain Rajput tribes in Western India; and the Jaina never attempted to save the countless children thus done to death. Concerning this the Government Gazetteer of the Bombay Presidency says with justifiable indignation:— "Brahmans who would not destroy the most hurtful reptile, and Jains, who cover their mouths that they may not injure the smallest insect, looked on with apathy from generation to generation, never raising their voice in behalf of the helpless creatures, who, year after year, were sacrificed at the shrine of superstition and pride." †

ix. Papa.

Eighteen kinds of Sin.

The ninth category deals with sin (*Pāpa* પાપ), of which, according to the Jaina, there are eighteen kinds. The greatest of all sins is the destruction of life (*Prāṇātipāta* પ્રાણાતિપાત), and this carries with it the heaviest punishment; the guilt increases in accordance with the number of "senses" the thing injured possesses (so that the greatest guilt is incurred by killing a man), and also in accordance with the motive from which the action was done. *Mriṣāvāda* (મૃષાવાદ), or telling lies, is also forbidden, but the truth should be spoken pleasantly. *Adattādāna* (અદત્તાદાન), or

* The exaggerated value Jaina place on *animal* rather than *human* life was clearly shewn in the famine. In more than one town they were seen to drive away starving little children from picking up scattered grains of corn, so that pigeons might get a full meal.

† Bombay Gazetteer, vol. viii. p. 112.

stealing, is prohibited in all its branches: one must not steal, receive stolen property, shelter a thief, or smuggle. Treason, curiously enough, is also forbidden under this head. The other Sins forbidden are *Abrahmacarya* (અબ્રહ્મચર્ય) or unchastity; *Parigraha* (પરિગ્રહ), or gathering possessions with too much greed; *Krodha* (ક્રોધ), anger; *Māna* (માન), or conceit; *Māyā* (માયા), or deceit; *Lobha* (લોભ), avarice; *Rāga* (રાગ), or overfondness for persons or things; *Dvesa* (દ્વેષ), or enmity (which includes envy, spite and maliciousness); *Kles'a* (કલેશ), quarrelsomeness; *Abhyākhyāna* (અભ્યાખ્યાન), slander; *Pais'unya* (પૈશુન્ય), or talebearing; *Parapravāda Nindā* (પરપ્રવાદ નિંદા), or fault finding; *Rati Arati* (રતિ અરતિ), lack of self control; *Māyāmrisā* (માયામૃષા), or *suggestio falsi*; and *Mithyādars'ana S'alya* (મિથ્યાદર્શન શલ્ય), or false faith.

All these eighteen sins are carefully tabulated as forbidden, but there is a curious passage in one of the new Jaina religious school books, which runs:—"Children, you must not commit such sins aimlessly, where no end can be gained for yourselves, and the interests of your relatives are not concerned; moreover sins should be kept within bounds." *

Results of sin.

Sin will hinder our attaining in our next birth to Right Knowledge, Faith and Conduct. For example, if a man is reborn wealthy, he may be unable to give alms owing to the miserliness produced by his sins in a past life.

---

* છોકરાઓ! જેમાં તમારો મતલબ ન સરતો હોય, તેમ તમારાં સગા સંબંધીનું કામ પણ ન હોય, તેવી નકામી રીતે તેવાં પાપ ન કરવાં જોઇએ, અને તેની મર્યાદા રાખવી જોઇએ.

જૈન ધર્મ પ્રવેશ પોથી. Part 2. p. 55.

Again one may, as the result of sin, become a beast or a bird, or be born in Hell. To be born in Hell is the worst of all punishments, while another of the heaviest penalties is to be born an onion or other " one-sensed " thing.

If in one life a woman is not faithful to her husband, she will in the next become a widow. It is hideous to think of all the suffering that has been caused by this one article of belief, and this suffering has been heightened by the fact that it is only the child widow, *i. e.* the one most incapable of defending herself, who is believed to have thus sinned. When older women lose their husbands in mature life, it is considered simply to be in the course of nature.

Certain other sins cause physical deformity in the next birth, or may make a woman childless. Loss of friends, relations, wealth, etc., are all put down to sins in a former life, as are excessive sleepiness and laziness. One Jaina gentleman told me that, as his family consisted only of daughters, he found it a great expense to marry them all off, but he dare not complain, as all his friends assured him it was only his just punishment for having misappropriated funds in a previous existence !

JAINA DIVISIONS OF TIME.

The Jaina believe that, while the world was never created and will never end, two periods of time, a Rise and a Decline, have followed each other and will follow each other endlessly in ceaseless rotation.

These two divisions are known as the *Utsarpiṇi* (ઉત્સર્પિણી), or Rising, and the *Avasarpiṇi* (અવસર્પિણી) or Falling; each of these, true to the Jaina genius for classification, is subdivided into six periods.

A Utsarpini.

This era begins when everything is at its very worst, and its first and worst period is known as *Duṣama Duṣama* (દુષમ દુષમ). This is followed by *Duṣama*, when, though everything is very evil, a sight improvement has taken place. *Duṣama Suṣama* (દુષમ સુષમ) is a period a little better still, when there is some joy as well as some sorrow; and in *Suṣama Duṣama* joy preponderates over sorrow. The fifth period, *Suṣama,* is entirely joyful, and it is followed by *Suṣama Suṣama*, a time of extreme and intense joy.

B. Avasarpini.

Unfortunately we are now living in the declining period of the world's happiness.

(1) It began with *Suṣama Suṣama*, a period which lasted for countless years, and of which a rather pretty picture was given me by a Jaina. The children that were born in that happy age were always fortunate. They were always born twins, a boy and girl, beautiful trees provided them with fruit to eat, and the bark of these trees served

them as garments. On the fourth day after their birth they were able to eat as much food as was equal to a grain of corn in size; they never ate a larger meal throughout their lives, and this meal they only took every fourth day. They never had to cook their food, but the desire-fulfilling tree, the Kalpa Vṛikṣa (કલ્પ વૃક્ષ), served their need. The parents died as soon as the children were forty-nine days old, and the children lived lives of such innocence that they did not even know what a dwelling place, a cooking utensil, cooked food, or religion were, and at their death this innocence took them to Devaloka.

(2) *Suṣama.* Happy twins were born in this period too, the differences being that they could eat on the third day after their birth, and continued to eat, every third day of their lives, a meal equal in size to a Bora (બોર), or jujube fruit, and the parents lived till their children were sixty-four days old. These twins, like the previous ones, went straight to Devaloka at death.

(3) *Suṣama Duṣama.* The twins that are born in this period eat every second day a meal the size of an A'maḷā (આમળા) fruit, and their parents live till their children are seventy-nine days old.

The first Jaina Tirthaṅkara, Ṛiṣabhadeva, took birth in the latter part of this period and taught the twins the seventy-two useful arts (*i. e.* cooking, sewing, pottery, carpentry, &c.). After this the happy times ceased, the desire-fulfilling trees disappeared, and fortunate twins were no longer born. Ṛiṣabhadeva also introduced politics and established a kingdom, and taught his daughters letters and the art of writing. Ṛiṣabhadeva's elder daughter, Brāhmi, is the Jaina patron of learning.

(4) *Duṣama Suṣama.* The remaining twenty-three Tirthaṅkara took birth in this period, which lasted for an ocean of time, and the Jaina religion was then fully developed. The people who were born in that age might at death go to any of the four states (*Gati*),* *i. e.*, might go to Hell or Heaven or become a man or a beast. A man of this period could generally eat thirty-two morsels of food, and a woman twenty-eight.

(5) *Duṣama.* This is the period in which we are at present living. It began three and a half years after Mahāvira reached Mokṣa, and will last for 21,000 years.

No one born in this period can reach Mokṣa in one life; however good an ascetic or a layman may be, he must undergo another birth. No Tirthaṅkara will be born during Duṣama, and no one will live longer than one hundred years. At the beginning of this period a man's height was seven cubits, but it is gradually decreasing.

We see another proof of the pessimism inherent in Jainism in their belief that during this period the Jaina faith will steadily decline, until at last it is quite extinct.

The last Jaina monk will be called Duppasaha Suri (દુપ્પસહ સુરિ), the last nun Falgus'ri (ફલ્ગુશ્રી), the last lay man Nāgila (નાગિલ) and the last lay woman Satyas'ri (સત્યશ્રી).

Thoughtful Jaina find this belief as to the imminent extinction of their faith a great bar to energetic action for the spread of Jainism.

(6) *Duṣama Duṣama.* This period will also last for 21,000 years. In the beginning of the epoch a man's life

---

* See Page 59.

will only last for sixteen years and will go on decreasing, and in the same way the average human height, at first only one cubit, will get smaller and smaller.

At the end of the period terrific winds will blow, rains fall and flames appear in such a violent storm that it will almost seem as if the world were going to be destroyed, but as the world is eternal, that of course cannot really happen. Animals and men will shrink to the size of seeds, and birds and the seeds of every plant will take refuge in the river Ganges, in the ocean, or in caves.

At last the time will come for the era of Utsarpiṇi to recommence, and a gradual improvement will set in: the seeds will grow, and in the third period the Jaina religion will begin afresh. In due course this era will again be followed by Avasarpiṇi, and so on in endless succession, as night follows day.

FIVE KINDS OF KNOWLEDGE.

The Jaina have a classification of knowledge on which they lay great stress, and which is believed to be peculiar to themselves. They divide it into five classes.

(1) *Mati Jñāna* (મતિ જ્ઞાન), which depends on making the right use of intellect and conscience.

(2) *S'ruta Jñāna* (શ્રુત જ્ઞાન), or knowledge attained by hearing, preaching and the reading of S'āstra, &c. This knowledge is intimately connected with knowledge of the previous class.

(3) *Avadhi Jñāna* (અવધિ જ્ઞાન). Limited knowledge of things beyond the ken of ordinary men, for instance knowledge concerning the heavens, gods, the actions of friends at a distance, &c.

(4) *Manaḥparyāya Jñāna* (મનઃપર્યાય જ્ઞાન). Knowledge of what passes in the minds of others.

(5) *Kevala Jñāna* (કેવલ જ્ઞાન). The perfect knowledge or omniscience possessed by the *Kevali*.

RATNA TRAYA.

The Jaina sum up all their rules of conduct and all their doctrines, with their multifarious subdivisions, under the name of the Three Jewels, or *Ratna Traya* (રત્ન ત્રય).

These are *Jñāna* (જ્ઞાન), or Right Knowledge of the Jaina doctrines; *Darśana* (દર્શન), or Right Faith in those doctrines; and *Cāritrya* (ચારિત્ર્ય), or Right Conduct in fulfilling the Jaina vows and duties; of these the first two are considered of no avail without the last.

It is interesting to notice in this connection that though the Buddhists also speak of Tri-ratna, or Three jewels, with them these terms denote three concrete things: Buddha, the Law and the Order.

JAINA WORSHIP.

The Jaina seem always to have chosen for their sanctuaries the crests of wooded hills. In Western India there are three shrines of special sanctity and beauty to which the S'vetāmbara and Digambara Jaina go on pilgrimage.

S'atrunjaya.

The most sacred of these, "the first of places of pilgrimage, the bridal hall of those who would marry everlasting rest," is the hill of S'atrunjaya, near Pālitāṇā in Kāṭhiāwāḍ. This hill, which is sacred to A'dinātha, rises to the height of some 1977 feet above sea level, and the summit is entirely covered with temples. "Street after street, and square after square, extend these shrines of the Jain faith, with their stately enclosures, half palace, half fortress, raised, in marble magnificence, upon the lonely and majestic mountain."* Indeed, so many are the temples, that to go round them all is said to require ninety-nine pilgrimages.

Girna'r.

Mount Girnār, (the hill of Neminātha), can be seen on a clear day from S'atrunjaya, to which it is only second in sanctity. It is situated in the Mahomedan State of Junāgaḍh, and its summit is gained by the most magnificent stairway in the world, flight upon flight of stone steps, which lead from the plain beneath, past the Neminātha fortress with its wealth of temples, to the highest of the five peaks, some 3,666 feet above the level of the sea.

---

* A. K. Forbes. Rās Mālā pp. 5, 6.

The Dilvārā temples on Mount A'bu, though they lack the surpassing sanctity of S'atrunjaya, and their site has not the wild grandeur of Girnār, are in themselves perhaps the most beautiful of all. A walk of about a mile through a pleasant valley connects the rising ground on which they stand with the little hill station of A'bu.

A'bu.

The larger shrines belong to the S'vetāmbara sect, and the brothers Vastupāla and Tejapāla—they died in the years A. D. 1242 and 1252 respectively—who had spent, it is said, eighteen crores of rupees in erecting the temples on the S'atrunjaya hills, spent twenty-four crores more on erecting temples here and on Girnār.

Digambara Morning Worship.

Across the way from these shrines is a little temple of the Digambara sect, which has lately been restored through the zeal of the Bombay Provincial Association of Digambara Jaina. Through the courtesy of their representative in A'bu, we were permitted to watch their morning and evening worship. Two steep flights of steps lead to the temple court, in the centre of which is a shrine of A'dinātha, and round the court are windowless cells, built for the occupation of visiting monks, nuns and pilgrims. There is an additional room with five or six separate hearths which serves as a kitchen.

We arrived about 8 A. M., and found the Jaina *Pujāri* taking an early cup of tea before beginning his work. After removing our shoes, we were allowed to stand on the floor before the door of the temple during the worship, which lasted about an hour and a half, and which consisted in cleansing the idols, marking them and offering rice. In the main circle of the temple, or Raṅga Maṇḍapa (રંગ મંડપ), were two figures of A'dinātha and two of Mahāvira.

In a furthur recess, the Gabhāro (ગભારો), which one might almost call a chancel, were two figures of Sambhavanātha, and within the inner shrine, the Sevāno Gabhāro (સેવાનો ગભારો), a larger figure of A'dinātha and his attendant Yakṣas, set in a background of beautiful carving.

The furniture of the temple consisted of a beautiful silvered alms chest or Bhaṇḍāra (ભંડાર), standing just in front of a rough wooden table on which was a square silver stand for the sacred book. Behind this table was a smaller wooden one, also bare, save for a three-legged stool which rested on it. A hanging brass bell and a moveable gong completed the equipment.

The images of the Tirthaṅkara were all of white marble and quite nude, wearing only a star-shaped ornament on their breasts. Just as with the S'vetāmbara, the figures are seated with their legs in the *Padmāsana* (પદ્માસન) posture, *i. e.* crossed in front, the toes of one foot resting close upon the knee of the other, and their hands in the *Kāusagga* position, *i. e.* the right hand over the left in the lap. The eyes of the Tirthaṅkara in the Digambara temples are devoutly cast down, in the S'vetāmbara they are staring straight in front of them. The Digambara lay great stress on this difference, as shewing how completely their Tirthaṅkara have renounced the world.*

* **It is interesting, however, to note, as perhaps indicating local divergencies, that in the plates illustrating Dr. Burgess' 'Digambara Jaina Inconography' the Tirthaṅkara are represented as nude iudeed, but looking straight in front of them.**

The *pujāri*, not being a monk, was unshaven and wore a moustache. In the adjoining temples the pujāri are Hindus and so take far less interest in the worship than the Jaina we had the opportunity of watching here; in fact we did not happen to meet in A'bu a single S'vetāmbara pujāri who knew the *S'loka* proper to the various acts of worship.

After bathing, the pujāri entered the shrine and washed the sacred vessels and the smaller wooden table in front of the large figure. Taking a duster, and regardless apparently of any small insects he might be killing, he cleaned the inner shrine with resounding whacks of his cloth and roughly swept the steps.

After having placed a little heap of yellow powder on the washed table, he proceeded to dust the figure of A'dinātha by dealing it several smacks on its face with his duster. Then, more reverently, he stood in front of the image and gently poured a little water on its forehead, mopping up the drops as they fell and wiping it all over, first with a damp and then with a dry cloth.

Both here and on Mount Girnār the Digambara pujāri were most careful lest any water should fall to the ground—they said that if even a drop fell, it would be accounted a sin—whereas the Svetāmbara were quite careless on this point.*

In the same way he wiped the marble of the inner shrine and then the other Tirthaṅkara in the body of the

* Dr. Burgess. however, in the book already mentioned gives as one of the differences between Digambaras and S'vetāmbaras that the former "bathe their images with abundance of water but the S'vetāmbaras use very little." Dig. Jaina Iconography, p. 2.

outer one; this done, he anointed and washed himself and his *loto** intoning all the time.

He then turned to the left corner of the temple, in which were a collection of beautifully polished brass vessels and the materials for the offering—rice, spices, almonds, etc., but no *fresh* fruit or flowers, which the Digambara, unlike the S'vetāmbara, may not offer. The rice he washed most thoroughly three or four times and drained off the water. Then he rubbed some saffron and sandal wood on a stone till he had made a yellow paste called Kes'ara (કેસર). Next he took up an empty brass tray and drew on it the *Svastika* 卐 sign with Kes'ara, and taking a vessel not unlike an upturned chalice, he marked it in the same way on what we should have called the base.

To the tray which held the rice he added spices, chopped cocoanut and uncracked almonds, arranging them all in separate little heaps.

Going to the little wooden table, he placed on it, and directly in front of the image, the upturned chalice and the empty 卐 marked tray, together with a cup.

He then filled two brass tumblers with a mixture of yellow powder and water, and placing in them two long-handled spoons and two very small bowls set them on the three legged stool; beneath this on the wooden table itself he placed the tray heaped with rice, etc., and then began a most interesting ceremony, mainly consisting of lifting grains of rice, etc., from the full tray and putting them on to the marked tray and chalice, to the accompaniment of elaborate genuflexions and intonings.

---

* A brass cup for holding water.

The pujāri completed his own preparations for this ceremony by taking off his vest, and, clothed only in his *dhoti*, or loin cloth, unwound the pagari from his head and arranged it over his bare shoulder like a *khesa*, or scarf. Taking some of the yellow powder, he marked with a *sāndalo* his forehead and his ears,* drew three lines on each arm, marked the middle of his chest and each side, and finally drew a line round his neck. Then, going outside with one of the sacred vessels, he bathed again.

His personal preparations over, he took the gong, and striking it once or twice, laid it on the table. Next he took a spoonful of the liquid from the tumbler and poured it over the rice on the tray, and then did the same with a tiny bowlful, afterwards bowing elaborately before the shrine. Rising he sang loudly *Jaya Jaya* (Victory, Victory!) and continued intoning in the same way as before.

He then took a few grains of rice from the full tray and placed them on the marked tray and on the upturned chalice.

Again he took, on a tiny brass platter, rather more rice from the full tray, elevated it, waved it slightly and emptied it out on to the marked tray. He repeated this several times, and then lighted the incense and knelt down.

Rising, he clapped his hands, took a few grains of rice, touched his forehead with them and put them on the upturned chalice.

He rang the gong for the second time and poured a spoonful of liquid on to the rice on the tray marked .

* The marking of the ear is peculiar to Jaina.

He next waved a little rice in his left hand, clicking the fingers of his right, and then wiped his hands elaborately.

Taking the ends of his *uttarāsana* or cloth, he tied them over his head in such a way as to cover his mouth,* and continued to transfer the rice, etc., little by little from the full tray to the marked one, elevating and waving it and dusting either the hand or the little platter by means of which he had transferred it.

A third time he rang the gong, and after pouring out the liquid, he clicked the fingers of his left hand.

Then he stood rigid before the shrine for a full minute in absolute silence, ceasing for the first time the intoning which he had maintained all through the cleansing, preparation and offering. Then, beginning his chant again, he bowed and knelt, and rising, continued ceremoniously transferring the rice from one tray to the other.

He rang the gong a fourth time, and clapped his hands and proceeded as before for several minutes.

Then he rang a fifth time, again clapped his hands, and after continuing to transfer rice for a minute or two longer, he poured the contents of the two tumblers on to the rice in the marked and now nearly filled tray.

Again he stood reverently silent, then bowed, and untied his *uttarāsana* from his mouth and knelt, touching the floor with his head.

Taking the marked tray, he waved it before a cocoanut, which he had placed by the side of a figure of A'dinātha at the left of the *Maṇḍapa*.

---

* Dr. Burgess, *loc. cit.*, however, says: "The Digambaras make their prayers after the usual Hindu fashion; the members of the other sect close their mouths or tie a cloth over their lips."

This done he returned to the table, shook the grains from the upturned chalice on to the tray, and the ceremony was complete.

He explained to us that the offering to the cocoanut was in order that all might be auspicious, and he also told us that the food that had been offered would be afterwards removed and eaten by a temple servant, and that no Digambara pujāri would eat any of it himself.

Evening Worship or A′rati.

About six o'clock we returned to see the evening worship.

This occupied only about ten minutes, and consisted in waving a light before the image in the shrine.

The pujāri, fully clothed and wearing an ordinary native cap, went to the shrine, before which one light was burning. He lighted the little five-fold lamp or A′rati, and then struck a gong, after which he solemnly and slowly waved the light from left to right for three or four minutes, intoning all the time. He next turned to the Maṇḍapa, and waved the light in front of the seated figure of A′dinātha on the right.

This done, he put the light on the three-legged stool, knelt down, and rising, struck a gong, to show that the service was ended.

S′veta′mbara Morning Worship.

Early next morning we presented ourselves at the gate of the S′vetāmbara temples across the way, and the temple attendants, after some little hesitation, courteously permitted us to view their worship also.

These famous temples are beautifully situated on rising ground overlooking a little valley, across which a pleasant stream meanders through meadows dotted with palms.

There are four main temples, arranged in the form of a cross, and their carved white marble domes and pillars are a miracle of fretted loveliness.

In the first temple we entered, that of the Kārigara, or artificers, we were interested to notice before the shrine of Pārs'vanātha blackened lamps and other obvious signs of the Hindu Feast of Lamps, or Divāli.* We were told, however, that at the last Jaina conference objection was raised to participation in a festival which led to the destuction of so much insect life.

Throughout all four temples we saw far more evidence of the influence of Hinduism than in the Digambara temple. In the entrance was a *Mātā*,† together with a large image of Hanumāna killing Rāvaṇa, and beside it an image of Bhairava.

*** Dr. Burgess, *loc. cit.*, however, gives as one of the differences between the sects that "the Digambaras bathe and worship their images during the night, but the S'vetāmbaras do not even light lamps in their temples, much less do they bathe or worship the images, lest in so doing they might thereby kill, or indirectly cause the death of, any living thing, for to do so during the night they regard as a great sin."**

Not only on Mount A'bu did we see traces of the festival lamps that had been burning the previous night, but at Ahmedabad in Haṭṭhisiṃha's temple (S'vetāmbara) an unprotected light burns all night before the figure of Dharmanātha.

† A type of Hindu goddess.

On either side of the Vastupāla temple was a red daubed image of Bhairava, and amongst the Tirthaṅkara in the courtyard that surrounds the central shrine of Neminātha was the figure (dressed in red skirt and blue silk *chadar*) of S'ankes'vari Mātā, the mother, we were assured, of all the Tirthaṅkara!

Inside the central shrine of the third temple we found the lap of the large metal image covered with a cloth, to show that it had been washed but not yet worshipped. Retracing our steps, we entered the principal temple, that of Vimala Shāha, which is said to date from A. D. 1032.

Here, too, was evidence of the all-pervading influence of Hinduism in the shape of a large image of the goddess Ambāji, which occupied a cell bigger than any of the Tirthaṅkara cells in the court surrounding the central shrine.

The temple is dedicated to A'dinātha, but beside his stone image it also contains two seated brass images, one of Naminātha and one of A'dinātha himself, and two standing figures of Pārs'vanātha.

The furniture consisted of a long alms-table in the centre and a smaller alms chest on the right, and on the left an empty brass throne, in front of which a most beautiful brass lamp was hanging. The whole of the interior, in striking contrast to the simple severity of the Digambara shrine, was disfigured by quantities of vulgar hanging glass shades and cheap mirrors. Two banners on either side bore the Svastika sign.

In contrast to the simple, unadorned Digambara figures, the images throughout the S'vetāmbara temples are given staring glass eyes, are adorned with jewels, and are represented as wearing loin cloths.*

Another difference between the two sects which we shall note later is in the number of markings the pujāri gives the image, while a still further point of difference is in the pujāri himself.

In the Digambara temples the pujāri is always a Jaina, a Vāṇiā by caste; in the S'vetāmbara temples he is generally a Hindu, sometimes a Māḷi (Gardener) by caste, sometimes a Kāṇabi (Farmer), a Brāhman, or a Bāroṭa (Bard). A further contrast is that the S'vetāmbara pujāri may himself eat the offering after the ceremony, the Digambara pujāri leaving it for the temple servant.

The cleansing of the temple and of the idol was very similar to what we had seen the previous morning, though owing to the number of small images of Tirthaṅkara six pujāris were employed instead of one.

The central shrine and its idol were first cleansed, then the figures in the cells round the court.

The image of the Hindu goddess Ambāji was undressed, bathed, and redressed behind a drawn curtain by the same attendant that bathed the large image of A'dinātha, who however sang entirely different s'loka to the two images.

When all the smaller Tirthaṅkara in the cells were cleansed and marked, the Pujāri returned to the central shrine and marked the large image of A'dinātha in fourteen

* It is therefore not quite accurate to say generally of Jaina statues:—"The images of the saints, statues of black or white marble, are represented as nude." Imperial Gazetteer of India. vol. I. p. 416. This is only true of Digambára statues.

places, *i. e.* right big toe, left big toe, right knee, left knee, right arm, left arm, right shoulder, left shoulder, forehead, head, centre of chest, centre of diaphragm, centre of stomach, and palm of the upper of the two crossed hands.

(The pujāri informed us that the Digambara only marked their images in three places).

Then, taking flowers from off the alms-chest, he arranged them round the image and proceeded to put on its jewellery, which he had taken off in order to wash the figure. This took some time, as the image wore a crown, a necklace, earrings, bracelets, armlets, and a girdle. All this time another pujāri outside was preparing the yellow powder for use in all four temples.

If outside worshippers had been present, a most curious ceremony might now have taken place, *viz.*, the auctioning of the *ghi* (or clarified butter). One against another they would have bid how much ghi they were willing to give, and the service would then have been performed for the benefit of the highest bidder.

No actual ghi changes hands, it is now simply the arbitrary symbol for the amount they are willing to pay. *e. g.* If a man says he will give ten maunds of ghi, he has actually to contribute twenty-five rupees. The price of this fictitious ghi is conventionally fixed at one anna a pound, a price which must have prevailed long ago, as the present market value is ten times that amount.

The offering made to the image may consist of rice and sweets, with the addition of fruit, such as oranges, bananas, or almonds.

The cheapest service, the *Sanātana Pujā* (સનાતન પૂજા) costs the worshipper $5\frac{1}{4}$ annas, the next cheapest, the *Pañcakalyāṇa Pujā* (પંચકલ્યાણુ પૂજા) costs $5\frac{1}{4}$ rupees.

The offering is transferred from one tray to another very much as it was in the Digambara temple.

As no outside worshippers happened to be present, nor was there, as in the Digambara temple, any committee to provide funds for a daily offering, the worship on this particular morning was very simple.

The pujāri, whose mouth and head had been covered all the time he was cleansing the images, etc., lighted the five-fold lamp (*A'rati* આરતી) filled with ghi, on the lower tray of which camphor was also burnt; a second pujāri beat a kettledrum in the court, another man struck a bell outside the shrine, a fourth sounded a gong inside it, and the principal pujāri himself rang a hand-bell with his left hand, whilst with his right he slowly waved the lamp in front of the image.

Replacing that, he picked up a single-light lamp (*Maṅgaḷadipa* મંગળદીપ) filled with ghi, with camphor also burning on its stand, and whilst he waved this, he continued to ring the hand-bell, the other pujāris likewise continuing *con amore* to beat the drum, strike the bell and sound the gong, the echoes reverberating amidst the beautiful arches. Finally above the din the pujāri loudly shouted "*Bas!*" (enough), and the service was at an end.

A noticeable point about the ceremony was that not one of the men taking part in it was a Jaina, or professed to believe in the service he was performing.

7

S'veta'mbara Evening Worship.

Haṭṭhisiṁha's temple in Ahmedabad is a modern Jaina sanctuary famous for its architectural beauty. Its façade, decorated with Ionic and Corinthian pillars, seems however curiously out of keeping with the rest of the building; and it is the entrance to this temple which is defaced by the notice: " Low-caste servants in attendance on visitors and dogs cannot be allowed to enter the temple."

Arriving at the time for evening worship, we were allowed to pass into the Gabhāro, where the worshippers were prostrating themselves before the idol.

The pujāri was, in this case, a Kaṇabi (or farmer) by caste. He lighted two little earthen lamps (kodiyāṁ કોડિયાં) in the Sevāno Gabhāro and placed them on candlesticks before the image of Dharmanātha (the 15th Tirthaṅkara); then, lighting two little sticks of incense, he placed them too before the image. Next he lit a little kodiyuṁ and placed it in the Gabhāro at the right of the door leading into the Sevāno Gabhāro and hung a brush of soft peacock's feathers on the door.

(A worshipper coming up at this moment was given an incense stick which he waved before the shrine; afterwards, putting that down, he took the brush of peacock feathers and waved that).

The pujāri proceeded to get ready the A'rati, and then the Maṅgaḷadipa (single light), by taking little portions of cotton wool, dipping them in ghi and putting them in the lamps, which were then lit.

A drum was beaten and two bells rung in different parts of the temple. A worshipper, who had offered a pice for the privilege, was handed the A'rati on a tray, whilst the Maṅgaḷadipa was placed on the threshold. This worshipper waved the A'rati from left to right; then, placing it on the threshold, he picked up the Maṅgaḷadipa and waved that in the same way, whilst the pujāri was chanting. This done, he replaced the Maṅgaḷadipa and waved the peacock feathers; the noise ceased, and the worshipper proceeded to say his private prayers, kneeling and prostrating himsef before the idol.

The lights, we were told, would be left to burn for an hour or two, in spite of the fact that, being unprotected, they were a grave source of danger to insect life.

Daily Worship of a Stha'nakava'si Jaina.

The members of the third sect of the Jaina, not possessing temples, and abhorring anything like idol worship, have no evening or morning worship similar to that of the Derāvāsi (*i. e.* S'vetāmbara and Digambara) Jaina.

A Sthānakavāsi Jaina layman, however, has most kindly furnished me with the following particulars of their daily religious duties.

Navaka'ra Mantra.

They should rise two hours before sunrise (though this is not always carried into actual practise in winter), and say the *Navakāra Mantra* (નવકાર મંત્ર), *i. e.* tell their beads (*Mālā* માળા), making salutation to the Five (*Pañca Parames'vara,* namely Arihanta, Siddha, A'cārya, Upādhyāya and Sādhu), and to Knowledge, Faith, Character and Austerity.*

* In Gujarat, however, most Sthānakavāsi Jaina do not include these last four in their repetition of the Navakāra Mantra.

Next he does *Paḍikamaṇuṁ* (પડીકમણું) either in the house or in a religious building.

Padikamanum. Paḍikamaṇuṁ has six parts :—

(1) *Sāmāyika* (સામાયિક). (See below).

(2) *Cauvisanththo* (ચઉવીસંથ્થો), which consists of praise to the twenty-four Tirthaṅkara.

(3) *Vandaṇā* (વંદણા) : salutation to the Guru, or, if he be not present, to the N. E. corner of the building.*

(4) *Paḍikamaṇuṁ* proper, or repetition of the twelve vows and confession of any infringement of them.

(5) *Kāusagga* (કાઉસગ્ગ) : sitting like Mahāvira with the mind lost in meditation, and secretly repeating *mantra.*

(6) *Pacakhāṇa* (પચખાણ) : taking a vow not to eat forbidden food during the day, or, if said in the afternoon, promising to abstain from the evening meal.

The *Sāmāyika* is generally said by Sthānakavāsi Jaina in a monastery (Upāsaro). On entering the monastery the worshipper says " Nisahi " (નીસહી), bidding worldly cares and thoughts " be-gone," and then, before beginning prayers, says " A'vasahi " (આવસહી) " Let me enter " [into what is necessary to be done].† Sāmāyika generally lasts about forty-eight minutes ; it consists of eight parts :—

Sa'ma'yika

(*a*) *Navakāra* (નવકાર), or salutation to the Five, as above ; (*b*) *Tikhuto* (તિખ્ખુતો), when the worshipper salutes the *Guru* (spiritual instructor) three times by moving his

* This is because Mahāvideha, the abode of the Tirthaṅkara, is supposed to lie in that direction. See p. 54.

† With the Derāvāsi Jaina, however, this word seems to be used differently, *i. e.* when about to resume worldly duties after worship.

hand or clothes from left to right. (If the Guru be absent, he salutes the North East corner in the same way); (c) *Iriyāvahi* (ઇરિયાવહી), or asking forgiveness for anything he may have killed when walking thither; (d) *Tasottari* (તસોત્તરી), the correct conduct which must be maintained during meditation; (e) *Logassa* (લોગસ્સ), or recital of verse in praise of the twenty-four Tirthaṅkara; (f) *Karemi Bhante* (કરેમિ ભંતે), when the worshipper promises to abstain from all sin; (g) *Namoththuṇa* (નમોત્થુણં), or general praise; and finally (h) *Sāmāyika Pālana* (સામાયિક પાલન), when the worshipper asks pardon for all the faults in his meditation.

Though a layman need only spend forty-eight minutes over Sāmāyika, an ascetic is expected to spend all his time in such meditation, though he need not do it exactly in this order. The reading of the sacred books is considered to be Sāmāyika.

Sometimes, when the layman reaches the Upāsaro, he finds a Sādhu preaching; and if he listen to him, that would be equivalent to doing Sāmāyika.

Before leaving the Upāsaro, he takes a vow with regard to his conduct during the day: that, for example, he will put on certain clothes, or use a particular bed, use only two chairs, or eat no more than five kinds of food.

He then goes about his daily avocations, but, like all Jaina, he must be careful to take his last meal by daylight, lest he should unwittingly kill any insect.

Evening Devotions.

After this meal he makes confession of the sins of the day, *Devasiya Paḍikamaṇuṁ*, (દેવસીય પડિક્કમણું), either in his house or in the Upāsaro, which must last as long as did the morning Paḍikamaṇuṁ.

This is followed by evening praise, *Sajhāya Stavana* (સઝાય સ્તવન), and lastly by a vow not to eat till sunrise, or *Covihāranām Pacakhāṇa* (ચોવિહારનાં પચખાણ). After this he is free to go home and please himself till bed time, when he must tell his beads and offer salutation to the Five before going to sleep.

Daily Worship of a S'veta'mbara Layman.

A S'vetāmbara Layman at Girnār was kind enough to give me some details of his daily worship, which we afterwards compared with the worship we saw performed in a little temple in Rājkot. The worshipper, we learnt, generally rose at seven A. M. and bathed, wearing a special dhoti, and his sacred thread round his waist, which Jaina (unlike Brahmans) only wear during worship. He might bathe either at home or at the temple, but he must be careful to choose a dry spot and to use as little water as possible.* After bathing, he donned, if he had time, the special seamless clothes (which are kept for worshippers in a room at the temple) consisting of either blanket or dhoti, *uttarāsana*, (ઉત્તરાસન) and an eight-fold *mukhakośa* (મુખકોષ), and marked his forehead with a cāndalo (ચાંદલો).

Vestments.

Next he walked three times round the temple—this is called *Pradakṣiṇā* (પ્રદક્ષિણા)—and whilst doing so meditated on the Three Jewels, and then entering the temple uttered thrice the "Nisahi" that bids all worldly cares begone.

Pradaksina'.

---

* Jaina are not supposed to bathe in rivers, tanks, lakes or the sea for fear of disturbing the water, but as a great many of them can swim, this prohibition is obviously often honoured in the breach.

The full ritual has eight parts, but the first rite, the *Jaḷa Pujā* (જળ પૂજા), or washing of the idol, can only be done once in the day, and so only one person has the opportunity of performing all the eight acts of worship. The actual pujā is very simple, consisting of washing the idol with sufficient water to remove all the *candana* marks of the previous day; instead of water, *Pañcāmṛita* (પંચામૃત) may be used,* which is compounded of pure milk, whey, Kes'ara, flowers and water. The idol is then rubbed over three times to dry it.

Jala Puja'.

This done, the worshipper proceeds to the next rite, the *Candana Pujā* (ચંદન પૂજા), or marking the idol with kes'ara. The use in Rājkot seemed to be to make only thirteen spots with this yellow substance, whereas in A'bu fourteen places on the images were thus marked.

Candana Puja'.

After that he does *Puṣpa Pujā* (પુષ્પ પૂજા), offering flowers and garlands. Other worshippers also do the Candana and the Puṣpa Pujā, till the idol is covered with various yellow spots at the appointed places, but as, before they can be performed, the worshippers must bathe and don the special dress, only those with leisure can do these rites.

Puspa Puja'.

To perform the remaining acts of worship it is not necessary to enter the innermost shrine, so ordinary dress may be worn; women also are permitted to perform them.

The fourth rite is the *Dhupa Pujā* (ધૂપ પૂજા), or waving of a lighted incense stick before the image.

Dhupa Puja'.

* Dr. Burgess however says: "The Digambaras wash their images with the *panchāmṛita*; but the others do not." Dig. Jaina Iconography, p. 3.

Dipa Puja'.

The fifth is *Dipa Pujā* (દીપ પૂજા), or waving a lamp before the shrine. As a part of this rite the five-fold A'rati may be waved, or the single Maṅgaḷadipa alone.

Aksata Puja'.

In the next, the *Akṣata Pujā* (અક્ષત પૂજા), rice is offered. The worshipper brings from his (or her) home some rice in a little bag generally elaborately embroidered. This he arranges either on the alms chest (Bhaṇḍāra) or on a stool in a particular form, thus :—

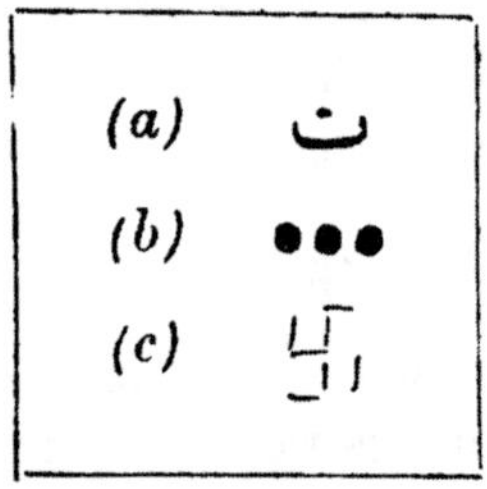

The Svastika sign (*c*) represents the *Gati* * in which one may be born, either as man or beast, in heaven or in hell. The three little heaps (*b*) represent the *Three Jewels* † of Right Knowledge, Right Faith and Right Conduct, by which one attains to *Mokṣa,* which is represented by the half moon sign (*a*). The rice thus arranged is left until some other worshipper requires the space for his Akṣata, when it is swept into the alms chest. At the end of a month all the rice in the chest is sold in the bazaar for the temple expenses, when, however, Jaina are careful not to buy it. Occasionally worshippers drop pice into the alms chest through the same aperture as that through which the rice is swept.

Naivedya.

The seventh Pujā consists of offering *Naivedya* (નૈવેદ્ય) or sweet meats.

Phala Puja'.

The eighth, *Phaḷa Pujā* (ફળ પૂજા), is the offering of fruit and nuts of all kinds : almonds, oranges, limes, bananas, etc. The pujāri

* See p. 59. † See p. 84.

eats such fruit as will not keep, the remainder being sold with the rice.

These various pujā need not be performed in any particular order, and the worshipper, if he be pressed for time, may only do two or three, in which case he will probably choose the Candana, Dhupa and Akṣata Pujā.

The method of performing each may differ with each worshipper. We watched one gentleman do the Dipa Pujā, after which, setting the little Maṅgaḷadipa in front of him, he did the Akṣata Pujā, and then, after censing his rosary, told his beads. He sang in Gujarāti the praises of the Twenty-four Tirthaṅkara from a little illustrated hymn-book,* which he had also censed. Each worshipper struck a gong when he had finished his pujā before leaving the temple, and said "A'vasahi" on entering on his wordly concerns once more.

If the worshipper had time, he might then go to the Upāsaro and hear a sermon.

In the evening about five he might go to the temple again to do the A'rati Pujā.

Sect Marks.

We were assured that S'vetāmbara did paint the sect marks on their foreheads; Dr. Burgess however notes in his list of the differences between the two sects: "The Digambaras paint on their forehead their caste marks but the S'vetāmbaras do not."† This would be true of the Sthānakavāsi, who never, in Western India at least, wear sect marks.

---

* As this hymn-book has pictures of all the twenty-four Tirthaṅkara, it enables the possessor to worship when it is not possible for him to go to a temple.

† Digāmbara Jaina Iconography. p. 3.

Daily Worship of a Digambara Layman.

A Digambara layman told me that, like members of the other two sects, he told his beads, but did not do either Paḍikamaṇuṁ or Sāmāyika. After telling his beads, he went to the temple about 8 A. M., and wearing only his dhoti did Kriyā Pujā (ક્રિયા પૂજા), *i. e.* offered rice, almonds and cocoanut. This took about an hour, and my informant did no more pujā during the day, because he happened to belong to the Terāpantha (તેરાપંથ) sub-sect* of the Digambara Jaina, who do not do A'rati pujā, giving as their reason that the Tirthaṅkara, having attained bliss, take no further interest in mortals, so that there could be no profit in performing such a ceremony as the A'rati. The Visapantha sect of Jaina, however, believe in offering the A'rati, for they say that, since the Tirthaṅkara, who have now attained Mokṣa, did so, there must be some advantage in it.

The Digambara do not permit their women to perform any pujā near the idol; they may only perform such pujā as can be done at a distance: (*Darśana* દર્શન).

---

* A Sthānakavāsi Sādhu kindly furnished me with the following information about the Terāpantha Sect.

They are recruited from all three sects, though their founder was a Sthānakavāsi, who about 150 years ago, in Sojat (Mārwār), entertained doubts about certain current practices, and founded a sect of his own. They are called Terāpantha, because the number of Sādhus who joined was originally thirteen. Their ascetics wear the same dress, etc., as the Sthānakavāsi Sādhu, but will not stay in an Upāsaro, preferring to beg the loan of houses from wealthy laymen.

The Terāpanthi accept the Sthānakavāsi scriptures, but read their own meaning into certain passages. They are not as particular as other Jaina about protecting animal life, never for instance interfering to save mice from cats, so the orthodox of all three sects unite in condemning them.

They are found chiefly in Kāthiāwār, Cutch and Rajputānā.

JAINA FESTIVALS AND FASTS.

Pajjusana.

To the Jaina of all three sects the most sacred season of all is Pajjusaṇa (પજ્જુસણ), or Paryuṣaṇa (પર્યુષણ, which closes their year. It extends from the last four days of the month of S'rāvaṇa to the first four of Bhādaravo (these eight days usually fall in August). Both S'vetāmbara and Digambara Jaina count eight days as the season, but as the Digambara keep seven days at its close for special worship, it really lasts fifteen days with them. The special object with which they keep Pajjusaṇa is to obtain pardon for the sins of the year. Every other day they fast and go to the Upāsaro, wearing their best clothes, while on the alternate days they eat specially dainty food.

The fifth day is conventionally celebrated as Mahāvira's birthday, though they know this not to be the true date. On this day both S'vetāmbara and Digambara go in procession though their towns, bearing an image which is generally that of Pārs'vanātha. The Sthānakavāsi Jaina would also like in many cases to observe Mahāvira's birthday, but their gurus frown on this, lest it should lead to idol worship.

On the fasting days the S'vetāmbara go to the Upāsaro to hear the Kalpa Sutra read in Māgadhi, the priest translating. The Sthānakavāsi Jaina, who do not accept the Kalpa Sutra, go to their own Upāsaro and hear Mahāvira's life read in their own Scriptures. The members of all the sects go to the Upāsarā as often as they can, and some of them spend the whole day there. A Jaina fast is exceedingly strict, for they are supposed to eat nothing at all, though they may drink water. Some very devout Jaina, instead of fasting on alternate days, fast for the whole eight, and some fast more or less for forty days. Their object in fasting is to gain merit and freedom from rebirth.

Poso.

Poṣo (પોષો) or Poṣadha (પોષધ). During Pajjusaṇa any Jaina may obtain special merit by behaving for twenty-four hours as an ascetic ;* during that time he wears old clothes and fasts, passing his time in meditation.

Samvatsari.

Saṁvatsari (સંવત્સરી). On the last day of the Jaina religious year all adult men and women must fast throughout the day. All through Pajjusaṇa devout Jaina have been doing Paḍikamaṇuṁ with greater zeal and attention than usual, but on this day every Jaina must do it. At the time of the ceremony all the temples are crowded; in large towns the temples have separate buildings for men and women, and the Sthānakavāsi have separate Upāsarā.

The *Guru* are present but they are making their own confessions privately, whilst some learned layman (or lay woman as the case may be) repeats *mantra* aloud in Māgadhi and afterwards in Gujarāti. This continues for about three hours; when the first person is tired, another takes up the repetition, and so on. The audience listen all the time in silence; they are supposed to be making private mental confession, but generally they simply listen to the *mantra*.

---

* The late Rev. Douglas Thornton seems in his able Essay (Pārsi, Jaina and Sikh. p. 62) to imply that this practise has fallen into desuetude, but this is not the case.

No light may be brought into the meeting, even if it goes on till eight or nine o'clock at night.

At the close of the three hours the lay people salute the gurus. Then they greet each other and ask forgiveness for any injuries or slights inflicted during the past year, and many old quarrels are actually made up at this time. If any one carries on a quarrel beyond Saṁvatsari and dies, he is in a parlous state. Going home they greet their non-Jaina friends and make up quarrels with them too, and they also at this season write letters to distant friends and put every thing right with them.

The Jaina are specially zealous during Pajjusaṇa to prevent any animal life being taken. In many States, such as, for instance, Limbaḍi, Jāmnagar and Morvi (in Kāthiāwād), they have prevailed on the respective Chiefs to prohibit all shooting, fishing or slaughter of animals during these eight days. In other States they try to prevent it for at least the first five days and the last by paying all the *S′ikāri* to remain idle.

Punema.

Four full moon days during the year are observed as special fasts by the Jaina. These days are called *Punema* (પુનેમ) or *Purṇimā* (પુર્ણિમા). The one that occurs about November is called *Kārttiki Punema* (કાર્તિકી પુનેમ); the next, about March, *Phāgaṇi Punema* (ફાગણી પુનેમ); *Caitri Punema* (ચૈત્રી પુનેમ) falls about April; and in June or July is *A′ṣāḍhi Punema* (આષાઢી પુનેમ). Both S′vetāmbara and Digambara Jaina decorate their temples with lamps on these days, and more of them than usual go to the temples to worship.

Oli.

In the month of March or April, eight days before *Caitri Punema*, *Oḷi* (ઓળી) or *A'mbela* (આંબેલ) is observed. At this time men and women take special vows with regard to the food they will eat, as that it shall consist only of one kind of grain for that day and that they will only drink boiled water. Women are specially particular in keeping these vows.

This, too, is the great season for pilgrimages; both S'vetāmbara and Digambara Jaina go on pilgrimage to Pālitāṇā, Samedshikhara (near Gāyā), A'bu or Girnār, where large fairs are held and the temples decorated.

Monthly Fasts.

A'thama and Pa'khi.

S'vetāmbara and Sthānakavāsi observe *A'ṭhama* (આઠમ), the eighth, and *Pākhi* (પાખી), the fifteenth day of each (lunar) month. Devout members of these sects fast, and all are supposed to go to the temples and Upāsarā.

A'thama and Caudas'a.

In the same way the Digambara sect observe the eighth day of the month, but instead of the fifteenth they keep the fourteenth day *Caudas'a* (ચૌદશ). Strict Digambara Jaina not only fast from all food on this day, but also from all water.

The S'vetāmbara and Digambara observe the anniversary of Mahāvira's birthday and the anniversary of the day on which he became a Kevali, but the Sthanakavāsi do not, neither do they keep two other festivals, *Siddha Chakra Pujā* (સિદ્ધ ચક્ર પૂજા) and *Jaḷa Jātrā* (જળ જાત્રા).

JAINA INSTITUTIONS.

Pa'njara'pola.

All three sects of Jaina unite in maintaining near many of the large towns and villages of India *Pāñjarāpoḷa* (પાંજરા-પોળ), or asylums for old and diseased animals.

Any one may send decrepit horses, cows, donkeys, etc., there, and the Jaina undertake to feed them. The pariah dogs, too, which haunt the streets of Indian cities, are often collected in vans and taken charge of temporarily, to save them from destruction by vigilant authorities.

Unfortunately these Pānjarāpoḷa are too often left in the hands of hirelings, without any proper supervision being exercised. The result is that they have earned a very bad reputation for starving and neglecting the imprisoned animals.*

Conferences.

Each of the three leading sects has its own Conference for the development and spread of its tenets.

The head offices of both the S'vetāmbara and Digambara Jaina are in Bombay, while the Sthānakavāsi have lately moved their head quarters from Morvi to Ajmere.

There are eighty-four subsects of Jaina, some of them differing very widely from each other, as the *Tapa Gaccha* (તપ ગચ્છ) and *Añcala Gaccha* (અંચલ ગચ્છ) do. The Sthānakavāsi claim to have very few subsects, but in all three cases the subsects attend the big Conference of their parent sect.

---

* One finds however that it is possible to secure some alleviation in their condition, if *public* attention be drawn to it.

The Jaina Young Men's Association of India has been formed with the object of promoting harmony between the three sects, and of furthering the cause of education and social improvement. They aim ultimately at the abolition of caste restrictions, the alleviation of the sufferings of child-widows and the introduction of other social reforms. But in these, as in all their other ambitions, they are much hindered by obscurantist priests and ascetics.

The pessimism which overshadowed the birth of Jainism still seems inherent in it, and its more thoughtful followers are not only perplexed by the conflict between its teachings and the discoveries of Modern Science, but are also discouraged from active effort by their belief that Jainism is doomed to disappear at the end of the present era.

INDEX.

Published by

Facsimile Publisher
Ashok Vihar, Delhi-110052 (India)
Website: www.facsimilepublisher.com

Distributed by

Gyan Books Pvt. Ltd.
5, Ansari Road, Daryaganj, New Delhi-110002 (India)
E-mail: books@gyanbooks.com, Website: www.gyanbooks.com

2 222000 013219